Praise for *Encounters with Heaven*

"For many years, Deacons Ensley and Herrmann have led parish missions throughout this country. Their ministry, Deacons in Ministry, has assisted many of the faithful to deepen their faith in Jesus. I am grateful to the two deacons for this continued ministry, and I pray that it will continue to bear great fruit. May we meet each day in our prayers and rejoice in the Lord always."
—**Most Reverend Stephen D. Parkes**, bishop of Savannah

"As I approach my seventy-fifth birthday, I find myself reflecting more on the end of life. This reflection is not something that worries or scares me, but it is one that is shrouded in mystery. I firmly believe in the resurrection of Jesus Christ, and I know that our loving Lord, who has brought me this far, will not abandon me at the end. Still, I cannot help but wonder what the end will be like.

"Thanks to Deacons Eddie Ensley and Robert Herrmann and their book *Encounters with Heaven*, I have found a new clarity about the transition from this life to the next and an abiding peace surrounding something that can be confusing, if not terrifying, for many of us. These captivating pages shed new light on one of life's great mysteries using biblical insights, Catholic doctrine, the witness of the saints, and the testimony of those who have experienced what it is like to sneak a peek into eternity. These insightful chapters will also help the reader to understand that those already 'beyond the veil' also sneak a peek into the here and now through visions and mystical experiences. I am grateful to Deacons Ensley and Herrmann for sharing their wisdom with us and for making my seventy-fifth birthday more enjoyable by reminding me that the end of life is indeed filled with light and that heaven is our true home."
—**Most Reverend John C. Wester**, archbishop of Santa Fe, New Mexico

"I love this book! And I think it is a most important topic for today, in this age of unbelief and indifference. There is very, very high interest (including my own) in what life after death could be like; perhaps one could even say, a fascination with the topic. This book has the potential to reach many otherwise unevangelized or lukewarm Christians with the gospel message of hope.

"Deacon Eddie is a competent student of early Church history. Both he and Deacon Robert have ample pastoral and teaching experience. In this book, they give a thorough and solid foundation to near-death experiences that Catholic readers (or any Christian) can be sure is orthodox."
—**Dan Almeter**, psychotherapist, shepherd of Alleluia Catholic Fellowship and moderator of the Alleluia School of Spiritual Direction

"As I read *Encounters with Heaven*, it was like drinking from a fountain that soaked my soul with happiness, hope, and a love that I never tasted before. It answered questions and blessed me more than words can describe. May God bless you as you turn these pages and open yourself to sights and images that are seemingly indescribable."
—**Dr. Richard G. Arno**, founder of the National Christian Counselors Association

"*Encounters with Heaven* can serve as a great consolation for people who have recently experienced deaths in their family or for those who are currently preparing for death themselves. I think the topic of near-death experiences presents an opportunity to address the teaching of the Church regarding end-of-life (eschatological) concerns, which this book succeeds in doing with gentleness, compassion, and understanding."
—**Fr. Matthew Mary Bartow, MFVA**, assistant chaplain, EWTN

"This powerful and brilliant book invites the reader to personally encounter the gift of heaven, the kingdom of God on earth as it is in heaven. Here we experience the spiritual journeys of many who encountered the spiritual universe beyond. The wealth of sacred inspiration here flows into the heart and soul as a gift of hope, healing, care, and eternal connection.

"Deacons Ensley and Herrmann offer a wealth of personal and historical reality as they focus on out-of-body and afterlife encounters. Clearly this insightful and deeply truthful book will open spiritual memories for the reader and foster care and love for others. This indeed provides a journey into the heart of God, a knowing beyond words."

—**Fr. Richard Berg, CSC**, psychologist, theologian, dean emeritus of the University of Portland, and author of *Scars*, a book on healing post-traumatic stress that was made into a Hollywood feature film by the same name

"A tremendous book to read and reread. As both a Catholic deacon and a person of Native heritage, I recognize the profound healing medicine contained in these pages. Where our ancestors spoke of the Great Spirit's presence in all things, these near-death encounters reveal Christ as the Light that transforms darkness into hope, isolation into communion, and fear into peace. The documented healings and life transformations bear witness to what our Church has always taught: God's love pursues us to death's threshold and beyond."

—**Deacon Larry M. Deschaine, PhD**, lead clergy for Catholic Native Americans, Diocese of Charleston

"Many years ago, I was teaching a course on the philosophy of religion at the University of Maryland. Since the course was part of an effort by the university to attract working-adult learners, our classes were held in the evenings. In the classroom next to mine, a professor was teaching a psychology course. On a break one evening, my colleague mentioned that she was beginning a module on the psychology of death and dying, including the phenomenon of near-death experiences. I remarked that my class was discussing the philosophy of death and dying, and that we should swap classes or combine them for those conversations. We did that, and it was a remarkably fruitful experience for all concerned.

"I was reminded of this experience when reading this wonderful book by Deacons Eddie Ensley and Robert Herrmann. Written in an engaging style, it is a balanced offering of spirituality, history, and theology. The stories shared are powerful witnesses to the love and transcendence of God, spiritual healing and conversion, and deep consolation. I found myself particularly drawn to the examples of near-death experiences and other 'encounters with heaven' throughout the Christian tradition.

"The authors' own pastoral and personal experiences add to this record of a wonderfully rich spirituality, and we owe a strong debt of gratitude

to the authors. I strongly recommend this outstanding work for all. It will challenge, inform, inspire, and console."
—**Deacon William T. Ditewig, PhD**, major theologian, professor of theology and religious studies, and former executive director, Secretariat for the Diaconate and Scripture, USCCB

"In reading *Encounters with Heaven*, I was filled with joy. I'll never forget the dying patient who told me one day that he saw death as an adventure. Deacon Eddie Ensley's books are always engaging and healing, and this one is no exception. It illustrates the great adventure that awaits us all. Reading *Encounters with Heaven* will take away any fear of dying and make you realize how deeply God loves you."
—**Judy Esway-Cugino**, Catholic chaplain and author of the bestselling book *Letting Go*

"*Encounters with Heaven* brings to light in a profound way what has been the experience of the Church—past and present—and of so many faith-filled Christians. God's promise of eternal life is a mystery but one for which God desires us to have an understanding and perhaps even a glimpse. This is confirmed by the plethora of witnesses who share their experiences. Thanks to the authors for their commitment to make this wisdom available to the ordinary person. This book is easy reading with profound insights."
—**Bishop Sam Jacobs**, bishop emeritus of Houma-Thibodaux, Louisiana

"Deacons Eddie and Robert masterfully craft this book, drawing on historical accounts from the saints and Church fathers, insights from scientific study, and recent occurrences entrusted to them by people they've encountered. We strongly recommend this inspiring book and are confident that you will find it difficult to put down!"
—**Sue and Ray Martell**, editors and resource managers for the US Catholic Indigenous Boarding School Accountability and Healing Project, authors of *Dreamcatching: Following in the Footsteps of Richard Twiss*, and editors of *Rescuing the Gospel from the Cowboys: A Native American Expression of the Jesus Way*

"As someone who experienced a glimpse of paradise from a hospital bed, encountering all my sins and God's mercy in one intuitive and overwhelming flash, this book is important to me. Late in my life it transformed my already serious Catholic faith into a mystical encounter that reduced me to tears of sorrow and joy all at once. It is here I find my greatest wisdom and strength. This is especially true during times in solitude and before the Eucharist.

"My experience is not unique. This book is a gold mine for those interested in this topic."
—**John Michael Talbot**, founder, spiritual father, and general minister of the Brothers and Sisters of Charity, Little Portion Hermitage

"This timely book by Deacons Eddie and Robert will be a blessing for all those who read it. Their decades of pastoral experience and their compassion for all those they encounter shine through these pages. The chapters deal with a topic that many ponder and question—and some perhaps approach with fear or trepidation. Deacons Eddie and Robert offer secure hope in God's faithful love for all his sons and daughters and our firm belief in the resurrection of Jesus.

"The healing power of God will never disappoint, and no one will leave untouched by reading and reflecting on the stories and the blessings included in this book. Deacon Eddie and I serve on the board of the US Catholic Indigenous Boarding Schools Accountability and Healing Project, so I am honored to endorse this work penned by my colleague Deacon Eddie along with Deacon Robert."
—**Mary Moore, STL**, director of Theology and Life Institute, St. Louis, Missouri

"Near-death experiences can be like shimmers of light from heaven to earth, intertwining with our human awareness, attempting to let us know that we are connected to God and loved and cared for by God, strengthening us in our ability to love him and those around us. The near-death experiences in *Encounters with Heaven* steer us into the ways of faith, hope, and love."
—**Sr. Mary Anne Schaenzer, SSND**, editor of *Pentecost Today*

"Deacons Eddie and Robert, both Native Americans, have opened the hearts of many to deepen their Catholic faith through books, preaching, and retreats. I have known Eddie for fifty-five years, and I believe these two deacons are profoundly mystical in their experience of the divine. In *Encounters with Heaven*, you will find writings from people throughout Catholic history who have had after-life experiences or visions of a loved one who has died, as well as memories shared with them by people they have known.

"If you ever question if there is an afterlife or if you wonder what happens when we die, you will find hope and a deeper faith in the mercy and profound love that God has for each one of us. I encourage you to read this book and find a renewal of inner peace."
—**Dr. Susan Sendelbach, MA, DMin**, pastoral counselor, director of Anchor Point Counseling Center, former Catholic and multi-faith chaplain, and former Catholic campus minister.

"These stories of God's saving presence are deeply moving and life-changing. *Encounters with Heaven* is a seminal work that will have a profound impact in the Church for generations. I can't wait to get hard copies of this book and make it available at my spiritual events. I have been waiting for such a book, having thought of writing it myself. But I could not have done as masterful a job as these authors have. I cannot overemphasize how important I think this book is. It will heal and save souls for many generations."
—**Rev. John Sumwalt**, Methodist theologian and author of *Shining Moments: Visions of the Holy in Ordinary Lives*

ENCOUNTERS
with
HEAVEN

Near-Death Experiences and Other Powerful Evidence of God's Radical Love

Deacon Eddie Ensley
Deacon Robert Herrmann

Copyright © 2025 Eddie Ensley and Robert Herrmann

All rights reserved.

Published by *The Word Among Us Press*
7115 Guilford Drive, Suite 100
Frederick, Maryland 21704
wau.org

29 28 27 26 25   1 2 3 4 5

ISBN: 978-1-59325-739-2

eISBN: 978-1-59325-740-8

Some of the stories in this book are based on true stories we have encountered over our thirty years in ministry. To maintain confidentiality, many of these names and some details have been changed. Any similarity to individuals known to readers is coincidental. The stories in which both first names and last are used are by people who wanted their names to be included.

Scripture quotations marked RSVCE are from the Revised Standard Version of the Bible: Catholic Edition copyright © 1965, 1966 National Council of the Churches of Christ in the United States of America. Used by permission. All rights reserved worldwide.

Scripture quotations marked NRSVCE are from the New Revised Standard Version of the Bible: Catholic Edition, copyright © 1989, 1993 National Council of the Churches of Christ in the United States of America. Used by permission. All rights reserved worldwide.

Cover design by Rose Audette

No part of this publication may be reproduced, stored in a retrieval system, or transmitted in any form or by any means—electronic, mechanical, photocopy, recording, or any other—except for brief quotations in printed reviews, without the prior permission of the author and publisher.

Library of Congress Control Number: 2025950640

Dedications

To the people who helped me in writing this book and spiritually gave me support during a serious physical illness that grew worse: Kathryn Jackson, Deacon Dewayne and Maureen Tillman, my pastor and Vicar General Fr. Scott Winchel, Fr. Richard Berg, Fr. Bryan O'Shaughnessy, John Cobis, Dr. George Capo, Ann Pinckney, Jackie Clermont, and my cousin Ernest Hale.
Thanks to my private editor Patrice Fagnant McArthur for her expert help, to Wayne and Vicki Scheer and Roseanne Maltese for their editing help and personal support, and to George Capo for his friendship.
And to Most Rev. Stephen D. Parkes, bishop of Savannah, for his love and support of our ministry.
—**Deacon Eddie Ensley**

For my beloved parents Irvin K. Herrmann and Hedwig Brenner-Herrmann. For indispensable love and values given.
—**Deacon Robert Herrmann**

Contents

Dedications 9

Foreword 13

Introduction 17

CHAPTER 1
Exploring Death-Related Visions 23

CHAPTER 2
Visions from Heaven in the Early, Medieval,
and Renaissance Church 29

CHAPTER 3
Communicating with Heaven 35

CHAPTER 4
Healing Visions 39

CHAPTER 5
Healing through Saintly Intercession 45

CHAPTER 6
Experiencing the Communion of Saints 49

CHAPTER 7
A Messenger of Love 57

CHAPTER 8
Lead, Kindly Light 61

CHAPTER 9
God Revealed 69

CHAPTER 10
Finding Our True Home 75

CHAPTER 11
How Near-Death Experiences Transform Lives...... 81

CHAPTER 12
What about Purgatory and Hell? 87

CHAPTER 13
Near-Death Experiences Are Real 95

CHAPTER 14
What Are Visions and Mystical Experiences? 101

CHAPTER 15
The Hope of the Resurrection...................................... 109

Afterword: A Look toward the Future............................113

Notes 115

About the Authors 117

Foreword

On June 1, 1989, my grandparents, Ernest and Marguerite, arrived at their summer cabin in the mountains of Colorado for their annual five-month stay. Their journey from Missouri had taken them not only seven hundred miles across the country but over seven thousand feet in elevation. They had made the ten-hour journey every summer for the previous ten years, always looking forward to the cooler temperatures, the beautiful scenery, and the excellent trout fishing in the area's lakes.

When my grandparents arrived that afternoon, they assessed the cabin for any winter damage, opened the windows to let in the fresh Colorado air, unpacked the car, and enjoyed a nice home-cooked dinner. Afterward they retired to the living room for a time of relaxation and conversation.

As the sun set over the western mountains, my grandmother walked to the window and stood gazing at the surrounding beauty: the trees on their property, the birds winding down for the night, and the chipmunks scurrying about. She said to my grandfather, "It sure is peaceful up here." Those were the last words my grandfather remembered his wife saying before she died that night: "It sure is peaceful up here."

My grandmother had experienced heart problems over the years and had a pacemaker from a previous heart attack, so it's likely that the long trip, the dramatic change in altitude, and the thinner air contributed to her passing at the age of seventy-seven.

I've often thought about that evening. Even though I wasn't there, I picture it vividly from my grandfather's retelling. I've wondered if her words were prophetic—speaking not only of the beauty outside the cabin window but also of the peace she was about to enter in eternal life. I like to think that she was being prepared for the transition from the brilliant beauty of this world to the indescribable glory of heaven—and that her final words echoed in both places: "It sure is peaceful up here."

Throughout human history, people have speculated about what lies on the other side of death's veil. To satisfy this curiosity, many have turned to various sources. We Christians look primarily to the Bible, the divinely inspired word of God. And Catholics in particular also look to the writings of canonized saints and mystics—individuals who had a special closeness to God and who were able to articulate their supernatural experiences for the benefit of future generations. These saints at times experienced divine conversations, visions, and messages, enjoying the rare privilege of glimpsing beyond the veil.

Scripture and the experiences of the saints whet our appetite and give us glimpses of the eternal, but their accounts are necessarily limited. Scripture often uses symbolic and poetic language when describing the heavenly realm. The saints and mystics, too, frequently speak in mystical terms that leave much to the imagination. While these sources may lead us to the threshold of eternal life, near-death experiences (NDEs) and out-of-body experiences (OBEs) sometimes carry us even further.

In the past twenty-five years, there has been a surge in stories of NDEs and OBEs. Some suggest these experiences occurred more often in earlier times than we realize, but people were less likely to share them for fear of ridicule. Others point to advances in modern medicine, which now allow healthcare professionals to resuscitate patients—thus enabling them to recall their limited experiences of eternity. Whatever the reason for this flurry of encounters with the afterlife, these stories do not disappoint. Indeed,

Foreword

they have borne the fruit of meditation and spiritual instruction on this all-important subject of the afterlife.

I am grateful for this book, and I hope it brings comfort, peace, and inspiration to all who read it. Deacon Eddie Ensley and Deacon Robert Herrmann's gifts as writers, pastoral ministers, retreat leaders, and ordained deacons in my diocese make this a work that invites the reader to ponder the mysterious, to journey with its characters, and to set one's eyes toward the beauty and love that God has prepared for those who love him.

I am so glad that Deacon Ensley and Deacon Hermmann lead us on this journey of experiences and stories from the lives of the saints, figures from early Christianity, as well as ordinary people. They document that in the Church tradition, thousands of everyday ordinary lay people had near- death experiences. From our own day, they tell the touching stories they have heard of life after death and the good things that God has prepared for those who love him. May these stories and experiences inspire us to be mindful of the goodness of the Lord and to seek to grow closer to him all the days of our lives.

Fr. J. Scott Winchel, vicar general, Diocese of Savannah, Georgia

Introduction

> If you read history, you will find that the Christians who did most for the present world were just those who thought most of the next.
>
> —C. S. Lewis, *Mere Christianity*[1]

Have you ever wanted to know what happens when you die? Have you heard of near-death experiences or deathbed visions and wondered if they are consistent with Church teaching?

Recent research has uncovered stories of thousands of people who have had near-death experiences, death-related visions, and glimpses of heaven. These all point to a remarkable encounter with heaven and a God who loves us beyond all measure.

"Overjoyed and Overwhelmed by His Love"

Jinny Oliver was in labor at St. Vincent's Hospital in New York City.

> As my labor progressed, I discovered that I was lying in a pool of blood. I became frightened as I realized that my bed was soaked in blood. When the nurse came in to check on me, she immediately rushed out of the room to call the doctor for the emergency: I was actively hemorrhaging. The nurses and doctor went into frantic action, performing a cut-down and pouring blood into my veins.

After a short while, I found that I had lost the ability to move or speak. I heard the doctor say, "We are losing her. I can't get a blood pressure reading."

After watching the medical team work for a while, I felt myself leave my body and hover near the ceiling at the corner of the labor room. I was not feeling any pain, and I was interested in observing the doctor's work on the body (which I knew was mine, although I was unconscious).

I traveled to the northeast (why this was important and why I remember it, I know not), out of the hospital. I was met by a light that was white and incredibly bright. It was whiter and more brilliant than any form of white we know on earth. Even though this brightness was just short of blinding and was brighter than the sun, it didn't hurt to look at it.

I perceived that in the light was a loving being. He came to welcome me and accompany me on the journey. I was with this loving being in a way so much deeper, fuller, and truer than it is possible to experience in this life. I was overjoyed and overwhelmed by his love. I don't have the words to describe this incomparable love. My human efforts are utterly incapable of communicating the reality of it all.

So many experiences followed: I instantly understood that everything in Scripture is absolutely true, and I had a very clear understanding of certain passages, such as, "For now we see in a mirror dimly..." (1 Corinthians 13:12, RSVCE).

I marveled at my complete understanding of complex theology and the profound spiritual writings of mystics. There was immediate, unspoken wisdom being passed from the Lord to me. I understood the why and wherefore of everything I might have previously questioned.

INTRODUCTION

I apologized for my past questioning and even my doubts. I was loved and forgiven as you might love a naughty little two-year-old child. Despite my sinfulness, I was loved and perhaps even loved more because I needed forgiveness so much.

I felt infused with wisdom, understanding, counsel, knowledge, fortitude, piety, and reverence—in other words, the gifts of the Holy Spirit.

Eventually, as I traveled with this heavenly being, we came to the great divide, a huge abyss. The angel asked me how I judged my life. It seemed that our final judgment is one that we make ourselves in the light of God's love.

I judged that I was not a bad person. I had tried to follow all the rules: I never ate meat on Fridays, and I never deliberately missed Mass on Sunday. My judgment was met by a contagious, wonderful laughter and an unspoken, "You got it all wrong!" Then he queried me, "But how have you loved?"

I was surprised and then had to admit that I certainly failed that test. I didn't know that I was supposed to love. I never truly realized the *raison d'être* of our existence! I had gotten it all wrong.

Despite all my very real awareness of my failures and sins, I was once again overcome with God's all-encompassing love. He loved me in spite of myself. I find it impossible to express the extent and depth and breadth and height of the love he has for each one of us and of which we are completely unaware!

When we came to the great divide, I was asked, "Do you want to go back to earth, or would you like to continue over the great abyss and on to eternal happiness?" Immediately I responded, "That's a silly question!" I couldn't leave all this wonder, beauty, and love to go back. He asked if I wasn't concerned about my husband and two little sons. My instant reply was, "They will do fine without me."

After experiencing God's love in an even deeper way (if that were possible), I realized that I had to go back. If we are gifted with all this love and I had not realized it while on earth, I must attempt to tell others. It dawned on me that Jesus deserves to be loved so much more than we do. I begged to come back so that I could "tell the people."

Without a look back or a goodbye, I found myself back in my body, lying in the labor room. I saw the sad look on the doctor's face. He was probably wondering how he would tell my husband that he had just lost his wife and baby. That look turned to hope as I opened my eyes and moved and my blood pressure started to rise. The medical team went into frantic action until my condition stabilized.

I still had many hours of difficult labor ahead of me, to deliver the now-still baby in my womb. I required nine pints of blood, suffered thrombophlebitis, and was kept in the hospital for three weeks to recuperate. Although my baby had died and there were moments when I deeply missed him, I was still overcome with feelings of happiness, remembering my remarkable journey. It was the most real experience of my life.

After such an extraordinary experience and because I begged to come back to "tell the people," one would expect that I would now be leading a saintly life. Sadly, I am my same old flawed self. And I don't preach from the rooftops, but I do share my experience with those whom I think may profit from it.

Over the years, I have been an extraordinary minister of the Eucharist in our local parish and when visiting the sick at their homes. I have worked in a local hospice as a social worker, and even if the message goes unspoken, I sense that people are given some hope and peace through my presence as they lay dying. I do find it frustrating not to be able to clearly explain my experience to friends and tell them to "wake up and believe," but I have found that is not always the loving way.

I try to live in the immense, indescribable, all-embracing, unconditional love God has for us. My hope and prayer is that we all respond to it by loving him and loving one another. And that we all one day will live together in his love in heaven.

Real-Life Stories of Heaven's Wonders

Experiences like Jinny's are much more common than was once thought. "There is currently more scientific evidence to the reality of near-death experiences (NDEs) than there is for how to effectively treat certain forms of cancer," states radiation oncologist Dr. Jeffrey Long, author of the groundbreaking book *Evidence of the Afterlife*.[2] Research reveals that near-death experiences were accepted and overseen by the Church Fathers and saints and often were accompanied by accounts of healing.

It is the authors' hope that these gripping stories from the past and today will provide powerful evidence of heaven and our ability to experience its peace even in this life. We can trust in God, who loves us, and in his promise of a beautiful life to come.

Chapter 1

Exploring Death-Related Visions

By Deacon Eddie Ensley

Over the last few decades, Deacon Robert and I have led hundreds of parish missions as well as weekend retreats for laypeople and clergy. During these preaching events, scores of people have told me privately of near encounters with deceased loved ones and others coming to them in glory.

"There's Light Everywhere"

A woman in her late twenties approached me after I had given a talk at a parish mission. She said that she wanted to tell me something. I was feeling congested and tired, but I reluctantly agreed, anticipating the story of a family problem or personal crisis.

The woman proceeded to tell me about her nine-year-old son who had died of leukemia a year before. Her husband couldn't deal with the illness, and he left six months before the boy died. But the woman wasn't telling me a tale of misery; a different kind of story emerged.

Toward the end of his life, her son told her, "Mama, I like it when I fall asleep, because every time I go to sleep, I go to be where Jesus is. There's light everywhere, and all the children laugh and play." Each night the boy told her more about the land of light where Jesus lived and welcomed him with open arms. That world her son journeyed to in his sleep became, as he put it, "more real than when you're awake."

One night, not long before the end, he raised himself up slowly and painfully in his hospital bed and said, "Mama, I know I'm going to die soon. I'm going to be with Jesus and play in the light."

The mother encircled his thin frame in her arms and wept, saying the only thing she could say repeatedly: "I love you, I love you..."

"Don't be sad, Mama. We'll still be in touch. Someday you will be with me."

He asked her to step back from the bed and bend down so he could touch her. "I live much of the time where the light glows and where Jesus is. I'm going to touch you now, and you can feel what it's like to be where the light is and where Jesus is."

The nine-year-old put both of his hands on her head, like a priest or rabbi giving a blessing. He held his little hands firmly on her head. She was overwhelmed by a radiant white light that she said seemed to embody love that is beyond conception.

Two days later, the boy died.

The woman said she was telling the story for me, not for her. She knew I was tired and struggling for inspiration to do the mission well. She told me the story of her son to encourage me.

Then the woman asked me to lower my head. She placed her hands on my head in silent prayer, the way her son had placed his hands on her. Unlike the mother, I did not see the light, but an unseen stream of brightness passed through me. I felt as though Jesus himself touched me, making me new. A cleanness and a refreshing grace washed over me.

Glimpses of Heaven

I had previously heard inspiring stories from people who had experienced light and seen loved ones from glory. I have even had such experiences myself. This story, however, was all-encompassing for me. I was stunned by the beauty of it. I felt the warmth of healing course through me, body and soul. Every bit of my soul was put at rest. The experience replaced my heart's sorrow with God's joy.

As I began sharing with people about the terminally ill son and his mother, people felt free to come forward and share their own experiences of death-related visions with me, many of them telling their stories for the first time. Some described being sped through a tunnel, where they witnessed a resplendent light that held the ineffable beauty of God's love. Often people informed me of meeting loved ones, friends, and family who had gone before them and who were surrounded by the light. These visitors came from the land of the light, which many called heaven.

Usually God would ask those having the near-death experience if they wanted to return to life on earth. Often they said yes and were sent back. Some who wanted to go on toward heaven were told there were things to do on earth, and they returned, sometimes with a message.

This woman's story also gave me a mission to aid other people: the gravely ill and their families, the bereaved and the fearful who deal with death. Such stories can also help people who are not in crisis step into the endless ocean of God's love.

A strong argument that such experiences should be given some degree of consideration are the long-term, positive transformations that take place in the people who experience them.

"The First Time I Prayed the Rosary"

Sue Martell shared this powerful story of a deathbed vision:

> I was raised a devout Protestant and converted to Catholicism as an adult. My husband and I live on the West Coast, and my parents live on the East Coast.
>
> My dad retired as chairman of the education department at a college affiliated with the United Presbyterian Church. He suffered a long battle with cancer. He was in hospice during my 2018 OCIA journey. My mom knew I was converting and was supportive, but she asked me not to tell Dad because, in the late stages of his illness, anything new or different would cause him to become agitated. I respected Mom's request.
>
> I wanted to pray powerfully for my dad—for his healing or for a peaceful passing. I asked my OCIA teacher if it was okay for me to pray the Rosary, though I was not yet confirmed. She said I could, and my husband, Ray, got one of the "How to Pray the Rosary" booklets for me from our church.
>
> I set aside a quiet time to pray my first Rosary. I stumbled over the unfamiliar process, but I strongly felt the presence of God in the room as I prayed. Later that afternoon, I was surprised to get a phone call from my dad. It was difficult for Dad to speak on the phone because the cancer had entered the bones in his face.
>
> Dad told me that a few hours before, he was amazed by the presence of a bright light in his room. He said it was a lady in the form of a beautiful ruby. God impressed on him that he should call me and ask who she was. I told him I believed it was a visitation of Our Lady—and he agreed with me. He had no idea that this encounter had happened at the same time I was praying the Rosary for the first time.

Dad died a few months later. I am still awed, blessed, and thankful that the Lord allowed me to share this experience with him.

In the following chapters, we will share more examples of these various types of visions and what they can tell us about the afterlife and the God who loves us beyond measure.

CHAPTER 2

Visions from Heaven in the Early, Medieval, and Renaissance Church

By Deacon Eddie Ensley

Determined to learn more about "glimpses of heaven," I embarked on two decades of research and found a slew of stories. One account comes from sixth-century Gaul. Gregory, bishop of Tours, shared the testimony of a simple-hearted holy person named Salvius.

Salvius had worked as an attorney but in midlife became a monk. After the abbot's death, Salvius was chosen to succeed him. He then became seriously ill. His fellow monks thought he had died and so proceeded with his funeral. On his death bier, Salvius awoke and said, "Lord, why have you brought me back?" Three or four days later, he told the monks of his near-death experience.

"When you saw me dead four days ago, . . . I was seized by two angels and carried to the heights of heaven." Salvius was then led to a place of "light unspeakable and unutterable space." Salvius' angel guided him until he came under a cloud "brighter than all light, from which came the noise of many waters." He smelled an "odor of exceeding sweetness." Martyrs and saints greeted Salvius.

After a while, Salvius heard a voice: "Let this man return to the world, for he is necessary to our Church." Salvius didn't like the idea. He said, "Lord, why did you show me these things if I must be sent back from them?"[3]

St. John Chrysostom's Thoughts on Visions and Grief

The great Church leaders of that early patristic era encouraged the bereaved to open themselves to visions of the deceased. St. John Chrysostom, the great father of the Eastern Church, wrote a consoling letter to a widow in troubled grief over the death of her husband.

Grief is important (in fact, Chrysostom had waited for a time before even writing this widow, aware that she must spend time grieving), but so too—after the first torrents of grief subside—is remembering that "death does not separate us from those we love." He encouraged her to let out her tears, then to remember the nearness of her departed husband. Chrysostom reminded the young woman that often God sends visions of departed loved ones:

> For such is the power of love, it embraces, and unites, and fastens together not only those who are present, and near, and visible but also those who are far-distant, and neither length of time, nor separation in space, nor anything else of that kind can break up and cut in pieces the affection of the soul....
>
> And if you find the trial very unbearable owing to its long duration, it may be that he will visit you by means of visions and converse with you as he was wont to do, and show you the face for which you yearn: let this be thy consolation taking the place of letters, though indeed it is far more definite than letters. For in the latter case there are but lines traced with the pen to look upon, but in the former you see the form of his face, and his gentle smile, his figure.[4]

Visions from Heaven in the Early, Medieval, and Renaissance Church

The Experiences of St. Ambrose and St. Gregory Nazianzen

St. Ambrose of Milan, who believed visions to be simply part of a believer's life, shared his anguish over the death of his brother Satyrus. Ambrose knew that grief must be expressed, even in public, if healing and cleansing are to come, and he wrote eloquently of his grief. But at times his deceased brother chose to come to Ambrose and comfort him. Ambrose wrote:

> How excruciating it would be unless [Satyrus'] image appeared to me as if here present, unless the visions of the mind represented him, whom physical eyes can no longer see. You are here... always presenting yourself at my side.... I embrace you, I gaze upon you, I speak to you, I caress you, and I am aware of your presence, in the very quiet of the night or in the clear light of day, when you choose to come back to see me and console me in my grief.[5]

St. Gregory Nazianzen also experienced visionary dreams of his departed brother. In a sermon of praise for his brother, Gregory talked about his own weakness in the face of loss, how difficult it can be to muster faith in the period of grieving. Yet even in that time of grieving, comfort can come, and awareness of the one lost can intrude.

In the midst of his very real human impotence in the face of death, Gregory looked to the time of the restoration of all creation, when he would see his brother in all his fullness, even as his visions and dreams anticipated that final seeing of the loved one who had departed:

> Why am I faint-hearted in my hopes? Why behave like a mere creature of a day? I await the voice of the Archangel, the last trumpet, the transformation of the heavens, the transfiguration of the earth, the liberation of the elements, the renovation of the universe. Then shall I see Caesarius himself, no longer in exile, no longer laid upon a bier, no longer the object of mourning and

pity, but brilliant, glorious, heavenly, such as in my dreams I have often beheld thee, dearest and most loving of brothers, pictured thus by my desire, if not by the very truth.[6]

Gregory also told of his sister Gorgonia's final illness. Physicians pronounced her illness incurable. During a brief remission of her disease, she went before the altar in the sanctuary to pray with "a mighty cry" to "the Physician of all." Her healing was to be a spiritual one, not a physical one.

Gorgonia had a "vision," as Gregory called it, in which she was made aware of the day of her death. Not only was she proven correct about this, but she was overcome by the beauty and goodness of God.[7]

St. Monica and St. Augustine

The words and example of St. Augustine—the great pastor, mystic, and theologian of the fourth century—are still a major influence on today's Church. Augustine was devoted to his mother, St. Monica, as she was to him. Indeed, it was her prayers and tears that brought Augustine from a dissolute youth to Christianity and later the office of bishop of the church in Hippo, North Africa.

St. Augustine had a mystical experience with his mother as she approached death. They were returning to North Africa after visiting Italy. In the port city of Ostia, they awaited their ship, which was to leave the next day. In the villa they were using at Ostia, they leaned out the window, talking pleasantly together, the garden lying before them. The climactic moment of Augustine's spiritual pilgrimage was a vision he and Monica then shared.

> But with the mouth of the heart wide open, we drank in the waters flowing from your spring on high, "the spring of life" (Ps. 35:10) which is with you. Sprinkled with this dew to the limit of our capacity, our minds attempted in some degree to reflect on so great a reality…

> Our minds were lifted up by an ardent affection towards eternal being itself. Step by step we climbed beyond all corporeal objects and the heaven itself, where sun, moon, and stars shed light on the earth. We ascended even further by internal reflection and dialogue and wonder at your works.... And we sighed..., as we returned to the noise of our human speech.... But what is to be compared to your word, Lord of our lives? It dwells in you without growing old and gives renewal to all things.[8]

Augustine and his beloved mother came near to touching, as he wrote, "the eternal wisdom which abides beyond all things," a wisdom that "alone could ravish and absorb and envelop in inward joys the person granted the vision. So too eternal life is of the quality of that moment of understanding after which we sighed."[9]

This spiritual experience was a shared near-death vision, for soon after this, Monica came down with a high fever and died. When Augustine became bishop of Hippo, he recorded many of the "innumerable" visions and miracles he witnessed or heard about from his congregation.

Hearing from Heaven

There are many examples of after-death communication in the Catholic tradition. Venerable Bede, the seventh-century historian of the Church in England, recounts one such story of a shepherd who was praying as he worked and as his fellow shepherds slept.

One night, while the other shepherds were sleeping and he was wide awake, he saw a long stream of light break through the darkness of the night, and in the midst of it "a company of the heavenly host descended to the earth."

They took someone of "surpassing brightness" and returned, without delay, to heaven. The other shepherds awoke, and he told them the story.

He told them, "I saw great angels descending from the door of heaven...." He described the angels taking a man to heaven and glory. He thought it must be "some holy bishop whom I saw carried to heaven."

In the morning the shepherd learned that Aidan, Bishop of the Church of Lindisfarne, a man of prayer and depth, had died. Aidan "ascended to the heavenly kingdom at the very moment of the vision. Immediately, therefore, the shepherd delivered over the sheep, which he was feeding, to their owners, and determined forthwith to enter a monastery."[10]

St. Teresa of Ávila's Experience

St. Teresa of Ávila, the great mystic whose life and writings have played a tremendous role in shaping the Church's spirituality, had a compelling near-death experience in her early twenties.

After joining the Carmelite order, Teresa became chronically ill. The illness was so serious that the sisters could not care for her, and they sent her home to her widowed father. Teresa fell into a coma that lasted four days.

> During that time they gave me the Sacrament of Unction, and from hour to hour, from moment to moment, thought I was dying; they did nothing but repeat the Creed to me, as though I could have understood any of it. There must have been times when they were sure I was dead, for afterwards I actually found some wax on my eyelids.[11]

Indeed, Teresa's fellow nuns thought she had died, though her father was less sure. One nearby convent went ahead and had a memorial service. Teresa awoke as she was being prepared for burial. She later wrote that the vision of heaven during those days was filled with a light so beautiful and bright it was beyond the telling of it. She saw Jesus' pierced hands, then his "radiant face."[12]

CHAPTER 3

Communicating with Heaven

By Deacon Eddie Ensley

In the last decade or so, studies on near-death experiences have broadened to include visions of loved ones and other people who have died "returning" to bring comfort to those left behind. These after-death communications (ADCs) may involve the senses of sight, hearing, touch, and even smell.

One study, conducted by Evelyn Elsaesser, estimates that 50 to 60 percent of the population have had such experiences.[13] We might conclude that these are not exceptional human experiences but in fact common, normal, and healthy ones.

A common experience is receiving a vision or hearing the voice of a departed loved one. Sometimes the vision is full of heavenly light, surrounding the person or emanating from them. Elsaesser's study found that these authentic experiences are spontaneous, instead of: allegedly initiated by the deceased, without intention or solicitation on the part of the experiencer, and direct, without the use of devices or an otherwise mediated contact.

Four hundred and sixty of Elsaesser's one thousand study participants had a visual experience: they saw the deceased. Thirty-four percent primarily experienced the sense of a deceased person.[14]

Visions of Loved Ones

Roseanne Maltese shares:

> It was one of those nights during the rainy season in the Peace Corps in Liberia. The thunder and wind had ceased, but the rain beat down on the roof of my house in Vezala. The boys who lived with me were sleeping, as was I. There was no music as lulling as the sound of rain on zinc.
>
> I woke with a jolt, existing in the space between consciousness and dreams, wide awake but unmoving. I heard a voice, soft and gentle, saying, "Roseanne, Roseanne, I love you," with such sincerity that it brought me to tears. The voice repeated, "I love you, Roseanne," echoing in the very core of my being. All I knew was that it was real, so I had to rise to write in my journal.
>
> The mail between Liberia and the States moved very slowly. About three weeks later, I received word that Poppy, my beloved grandfather, the person to whom I was closest in the world, had died. Though he had no religious connections, no belief in the afterlife, he had come to me to say goodbye.

As I reflected on Roseanne's story, I thought of her grandfather. Though he had no religious connection, he possessed a powerful ability to love, so much so that his love profoundly affected his granddaughter and likely others too.

A Visit from the Blessed Mother

Ann Pinckney, granddaughter of the visionary and retired executive director of evangelization for the Diocese of Savannah, wrote:

> My grandmother Schano (Granny) taught me about suffering with grace and the power of prayer. She had rheumatoid arthritis,

which was extremely painful and caused disfigurement of her hands and feet. In her younger years, Granny was very much a "church lady." She was a mother to four, secretary at two parishes, head of the Council of Catholic Women, and member of a few sodalities.

In the 1960s, Granny had an experimental surgery on her knees, in the hope she would be able to walk better. But she was bedridden within three years. Granny prayed the Rosary constantly, and I never heard her complain. She taught me to pray for people who had worse afflictions.

In the summer of 1969, when I was eleven, my parents trusted me to be Granny's caregiver for two months. I had to feed her, wash her, dress her, put her on and off a bedpan, and do light physical therapy. This changed my life and gave me great empathy for those who suffer. My family then moved to Savannah, and Granny moved in with us. She lived with us for a little over one year.

I do not remember how, but Granny came to be so sick as to be hospitalized and near death. My mother asked if I wanted to be present when the priest gave Granny the Sacrament of Extreme Unction, today called the Anointing of the Sick. On the way to the hospital, my mother relayed to me something Granny had told her: the Blessed Mother had appeared at the foot of Granny's bed and told her she would be with her in heaven the next day.

I certainly believed it. Granny had to have had a loving, bonded relationship with Mary.

It was a privilege to be present at Granny's anointing. She was at peace and no longer in pain. I knew the Blessed Mother was going to take Granny with her.

Granny passed away that night in her sleep. This event, more than any in my life, has shaped my views on heaven and the power of prayer.

Be encouraged, all we who hope for life after death in the presence of a just and benevolent God.

Phone Calls from Beyond

Judy Esway, a Catholic chaplain and grief specialist, wrote the popular book on grieving, *Letting Go*. She shared this experience:

> I was called as a chaplain to a room where the patient had just died. His wife of many years, his daughter, and many others were at his bedside. They asked me to pray.
>
> We gathered around the man, and I started to pray. When we heard a phone ring, everyone ignored it, not wanting to interrupt the prayer. After many rings, the phone stopped, only to start ringing again.
>
> I noticed the patient's daughter quietly leaving the circle. She went to the couch and rummaged through her mother's purse to retrieve her mother's cell phone. The ringing had stopped again.
>
> The daughter returned to the circle. I stopped praying because of the look on her face, which worried me. I said, "Are you okay? What's wrong?" She answered, "My dad just called my mom . . . twice." All of us were astounded.

I researched phone encounters such as these in the studies of deceased loved ones who have shown their presence. Experts reported that phone calls from the beloved are not uncommon. One researcher found fifty calls similar to Judy's encounter.

Hilda, still grieving the loss of her husband after many years, answered a call. It was her husband. "I love you." The voice was unmistakably his. He spoke in Polish, the only language he had ever used. Hilda's daughter witnessed the call.[15]

Chapter 4

Healing Visions

By Deacon Eddie Ensley

Many who have experienced death-related visions have reported a sense of healing as a result of them. In 1991, while leading a retreat in Alberta, Canada, I listened to a middle-aged woman describe her experience. She was a Catholic of Native American descent, and her words came slowly and carefully.

Years before, when the woman was young and living on a reserve, a teenage nephew whom she especially loved killed himself. He stole beer from her cabinet, got drunk, and drove off the road. The woman blamed herself. She fell into a profound depression that seemed untouched by counseling and medication. Her marriage failed, and her children chose to live with her husband. For years she lived in the misery of this tragedy.

One day, as the woman was driving to the grocery store, a tingling filled her ears, ringing inside and out. This puzzled her. She knew she was moving into the unknown. She pulled off the road into a clump of trees and leaned back in her seat.

She felt herself whisked out of her car and carried to a place of unspeakable splendor and brilliance. The awareness of Gitchee Manitou—the Great

Mystery, the Great Spirit of Native Americans—washed over her. Above her head she sensed a presence. When she looked up, she saw the hand of a healer holding an eagle feather. The healer sang an ineffable Christian hymn in her Native language that touched her hidden, lonely places with loving-kindness, carrying a power that strengthened her heart.

The woman turned to see what great healer held the eagle feather. She saw her nephew surrounded by radiance. Beside him stood Christ, who was holding the eagle feather. A flood of deep consolation burst forth in her body and her soul.

After returning to everyday awareness, the woman sat in her car and wept for a long time. Cleansed by this period of grieving, she rested in stillness. The vision marked a turning point.

The woman began to rebuild her life. This took time and much hard work, but she was able to begin anew because God had broken through her depression and guilt.

Deep Healing for a Grieving Widower

Throughout my thirty years of giving parish missions and retreats, I have heard many people recount what can only be called miracles. One miracle involved Kevin, a retired dentist in his mid-sixties who came reluctantly to a parish mission Deacon Herrmann and I led in the northeast. He came only because a friend pressured him to do so.

Kevin's late wife, Nora, had been the world to him. They had no children, but that never mattered; they found rich companionship in each other. Nora was a devout believer, but Kevin was not.

One day in their car, they passed a demolition site where a wrecking ball tore away at an old building. Just as their vehicle passed near the site, the wrecking ball tumbled out of control. It hit Nora's side of the vehicle, killing her instantly. Kevin's only family was lost in a second.

Kevin found himself alone, forsaken, and with little to live for. It was almost as though he were consigned to solitary confinement, with hardly anyone or anything to warm his heart. If there were a God, how could he let something so tragic happen? He decided that he would prefer to believe there was no God than to view God as a monster who took away his wife.

So here was Kevin, reluctantly, at the parish mission. The first night he attended, I led the group in guided stillness and imagery prayer. I had them imagine that Jesus was seated beside them, taking their hands in his. I asked the group to feel the place in his hand where the nail had been. I encouraged them to feel the healing warmth of Jesus' love pass from his hand to theirs and fill them, body and soul, with Jesus' soothing warmth.

I could see Kevin's muscles relax as I spoke of Jesus holding his hand. From the look on his face, I sensed that he was being drawn deeply into the meditation. I heard him make a guttural sound and, just above a whisper, say "no" twice. Then he opened his eyes.

Kevin recounted his experience to me the next night. He said he had felt Jesus come close to him, comforting him, the first comfort he had felt since his wife's death. Then he pulled himself back from the nearness of Jesus and opened his eyes. He couldn't let himself believe in what he thought was an illusion; he had to push God away.

That night Kevin had a vivid dream that was "realer than real," as he put it. His wife, breathing and living, surrounded by light, walked into his room. He said, "I could see the light in all my own cells." Nora came up close to him and brushed his forehead with her hand. A sense of awe, comfort, and wonder passed through Kevin. She was there, real as his heart, which was now beating rapidly in his chest.

"I've missed you so much," he said to her.

She smiled and said, "I love you and miss you too." She then looked at the open door to the bedroom and said, "Here is someone I want you to meet."

Kevin looked at the door. Jesus, surrounded by heavenly brightness, walked in, stood beside the bed, and comforted him with a hand on his forehead.

"Don't fear me, Kevin," Jesus said. "I suffered with you in your loneliness and isolation, and I am always here to help you. Come to me often."

Then Nora and Jesus disappeared. Kevin wasn't sure if it had all been a dream, but if it was, he said, it was a dream more alive than life itself. Whether asleep or awake, he knew Jesus had visited him and that his life would never be the same. He said again, "I could see the light in all my cells."

Kevin began attending Mass regularly, coming to the sacraments, and developing a prayer relationship with Jesus. He joined the Knights of Columbus, a fraternal organization for Catholic men, and established several sustaining spiritual friendships. He often told the story of his "miracle," which set his feet on the pathway into God and with God.

"I No Longer Fear Death"

At another retreat, Jason, in early middle age, came forward to tell me about his wife, Ella, who had died of breast cancer the year before. The doctors had stopped treatment because it was no longer helpful, though it had been keeping Ella alive. She went into hospice care and waited at home for the inevitable.

Ella was a caring person but a constant worrier. She voiced her fears to Jason and their teenagers: "I love you all so much and am anguished about leaving you." The deep creases on her face indicated the depth of her anxiety.

When Ella fell hard into a sleep that turned into a coma, Jason thought this was the end. To his surprise, after two hours Ella awoke. Her lips curled upward into a big smile. The worrying lines on her face had disappeared. "Radiant," Jason said, was the only word that could describe her demeanor. Ella said,

> I was surrounded by a living, brilliant light that profoundly calmed me. The light filled me with unlimited love and genuine joy. Words

fail me. I felt unsullied, calm, and relieved. I just wanted to remain there forever and ever.

The next thing I knew, my life was flickering in front of my eyes—everything that I had ever thought or experienced. I believe that in the light was Jesus and that I had surely glimpsed the light of heaven. I no longer fear death.

Ella's parents and her best friend from high school, all deceased, had come to her. From the light and from her loved ones, she felt a richness of love that she had never thought possible. She saw strings of love as strings of light passing from her body, surrounding her family. This light shimmered brightly and filled her to the brim with unshakable love and joy. And there were angels.

Ella told her family again, "I no longer fear death." Jason nodded and said, "And no longer do we."

Ella lived several more days. During that time, she often raised her arms as if beckoning beings the family could not see. "Angels and loved ones," she explained. She died, smiling and radiant.

From time to time, Ella visited her husband in his dreams. They would talk about how God is always near. Jason lost his fear of death, and his life flourished. The love that had surrounded Ella found its way deep inside.

Ella and Jason's children also prospered. The family shared their love by getting involved with a homeless shelter, demonstrating that the love and healing conveyed in these near-death experiences have the power to transform our lives here on earth.

The resounding message of both tradition and modern research is that near-death experiences hold the potential to lead us on a powerful journey of healing, both for ourselves and for those we care about. They open us to the One who can mend our wounds, change us, and send us out into the world with a love that mirrors God's own transforming love.

CHAPTER 5

HEALING THROUGH SAINTLY INTERCESSION

Church history tells us of many healing encounters with departed saints. They too are loved ones who have gone before us. St. Augustine includes several accounts in his masterpiece, *The City of God*.

St. Stephen, Pray for Us

Innocentia, a wealthy and prominent Catholic woman, had breast cancer. Despite receiving the best medical care available, her condition worsened, and her doctor told her that she had only weeks to live. It was Lent, and she prayed fervently.

One night Innocentia had a dream giving specific directions, probably from St. Stephen. She was to attend the Easter Vigil Mass at the shrine of St. Stephen, wait for the first woman to emerge from the baptismal font, and ask this new Christian to make the Sign of the Cross over her cancerous breast. Innocentia followed these instructions and reported being fully healed.

After a medical examination confirmed her perfect health, her physician eagerly asked what remedy she had used. When she explained, he dismissively replied, "I thought you would tell me something major." She countered, "Is it hard for Christ to heal cancer when he raised a man who had been dead for four days?"

When St. Augustine, the local bishop at that time, heard about Innocentia's healing, he was upset that it hadn't been publicized. On learning that even the woman's friends were unaware of her story, he made Innocentia share it with them.[16]

Augustine recounted this in *The City of God* to emphasize the importance of testifying to God's works. He knew that sharing Christ's miracles glorifies God, boosts faith, and inspires praise and thanksgiving, as it did for Innocentia's friends. While there can be reasons to refrain from publicizing a healing, generally it is right to give glory to God by sharing the marvelous things he has done. As the psalmist exclaims:

> I have told the glad news of deliverance
> > in the great congregation;
> see, I have not restrained my lips,
> > as you know, O LORD.
> I have not hidden your saving help within my heart,
> > I have spoken of your faithfulness and your salvation;
> I have not concealed your steadfast love and your faithfulness
> > from the great congregation. (Psalm 40:9-10, NRSVCE)

Such jubilation was evident in another instance of St. Stephen's intercession. Two young people, Paulus and his sister Palladia, suffered from a neurological disorder that caused trembling and convulsions. Through a vivid dream, likely involving St. Stephen, they felt a calling to go to the Basilica of St. Stephen in Hippo. There, they were told, they would be healed.

At the beginning of the Mass, Paulus prayed for a cure. He fell prostrate as though in a trance. "Just as suddenly," Augustine reported, "[Paulus] arose. The trembling had stopped. The whole church soon rang with the clamor of rejoicing. Nearly everyone broke into loud prayers of thanksgiving.... Augustine approached Paulus to receive the kiss of peace. "Cries of joy rose up everywhere. No tongue was silent."

The young man stood still without trembling, while his sister was still trembling and going into convulsions. The congregation prayed fervently for the healing of Palladia. Then Augustine dismissed the pair.

Palladia immediately went to a shrine in the basilica. Suddenly a new joyful song emerged from people in that area. Palladia had fallen prostrate, as though in a deep sleep, and arisen cured.

Augustine described the jubilation: "The exultation continued, and the wordless praise to God was shouted so loud that my ears could barely stand the din." But the main point, Augustine said, "was that in the hearts of this clamoring crowd burned that faith in Christ for which the martyr Saint Stephen had shed his blood."[17]

Ministers of Healing

There are hundreds of scenes in Church history where healing came from saints. They too are loved ones who have gone before us.

For example, a young Franciscan from a wealthy family disliked his uncomfortable habit and life of poverty. Seeking help from God, he had a vision of a recently deceased Franciscan known for his care for the poor and disabled. Inspired by this vision, the young Franciscan experienced a profound conversion. He embraced his commitment to the Franciscan life and was emotionally healed and transformed.

A fifteen-year-old girl named Anne experienced saintly aid in the year 1303. As a result of an accident, Anne's leg was crippled, putrid, and full of pus. Her father had begged for money to buy a wheelbarrow, and he carted her from their home in London to Hereford, where there was a shrine of St. Thomas. The family prayed day and night, begging for healing.

One night Anne had a dream of a kindly man with snow-white hair who carried the Eucharist. He came to her and anointed her leg. Anne raised her arms and shouted, "St. Thomas, have mercy on me."

The man made the Sign of the Cross on Anne's forehead. When she woke up, she was cured and able to walk.

These stories are among thousands in which ordinary Catholics experienced saintly appearances. Especially during the medieval period, many ordinary people reported wondrous visions of saints and those considered saints. Such visions would often occur when people needed healing, and the vision would tell people where to go and what to do to receive healing. This often meant going to a shrine where they prayed with others. And whenever someone experienced healing, they would go to a shrine to give thanks.

These encounters enhanced their sense of identity before God and community connectedness. Pilgrimages and visionary experiences helped unite society around the sacred. These healing and hopeful stories have been preserved through generations—being told, written down, retold, and passed down to children.

This tradition continues in places like Lourdes and Santiago de Compostela. Sr. Benedicta Ward, an Anglican nun famous for medieval and theological scholarship, states that early shrine documents show no signs of fraud. Those who recorded miracles genuinely believed in their truth. According to Ward, "All that can be said is that here are events that caused wonder and awe and were interpreted . . . as signs of the action of God in human affairs."[18]

CHAPTER 6

Experiencing the Communion of Saints

By Deacon Eddie Ensley

The Church's doctrine of the communion of saints affirms that all the faithful, both living and deceased, are spiritually united in Christ. In this sacred communion, the bonds of love and prayer transcend the barriers of time and space, allowing the living to remain connected with their departed loved ones in a deeply meaningful way. In this divine fellowship, the faithful can find comfort and solace.

We pray for our departed loved ones, and we know that they continue to intercede for us. Some people have experienced this in extraordinary ways.

A Family Gathering

Though experienced by a Protestant, this is one of the finest contemporary stories of the communion of saints I have ever heard. Robert Berry, my Native American cousin, shared this with me:

> Several years ago, I took off down to South Carolina to visit my friend Tommy. While I was there, I went deer hunting and processed

some deer meat. After working day and night, I became exhausted and experienced serious pain.

I was getting only three or four hours of sleep at night. One night my eyes began to cross and my arm hurt. Lying on Tommy's sofa, I fell into a profoundly deep sleep, or so I thought. I found myself being transported through space as an unseen man spoke from behind me concerning my destination. I later wondered if this was an angel.

"Robert," he said, "you are going to like where you are going, and when you get there, you will need to get in line at the foot of a stairway, where you will be joining members of your family."

As I traveled upward past the moon, stars, and planets, I was speechless, exhilarated, and filled with expectation—like a child waiting to open my Christmas presents, and the universe was my present. Never would I have dreamed of taking a journey like this one. I was in awe of the majestic creation that I was a small part of.

As I continued my trek upward toward what I did not know, time seemed to fly. I found myself halfway up the stairs when I realized everyone had left the line to be with their families, who were sitting at multicolored marble picnic tables. It was then that I noticed my family: my mom, dad, aunts, uncles, grandparents, great-grandparents—some of whom I had only seen photos of. Yet they were not strangers. Each one stood and walked over to greet me with smiles, hugs, and handshakes, calling me by name.

My dad, "Bill," as most people called him, said, "Son, I didn't expect to see you here so soon." Dad's appearance was that of a forty-year-old man.

My mom, Helen, ran over to hug me. Mom also looked to be in her forties. She said, "Son, I am so glad to see you. I missed you so much. I love you."

Dad picked up the conversation again. "Your mom and I have been watching over you."

As I gazed into their eyes, I couldn't believe mine. My parents were alive, and I was touching them after so many years, hugging them tightly. I never wanted to let them go. We were together again. And with happy tears streaming down my cheeks, I sobbed, "I love you, Mom and Dad. I can't believe we're together again."

Seeing Granny brought back memories of the last day I spent with her. She was on her deathbed, and I wanted to go in and share a grapefruit with her. Mom tried to keep me out of her room because she thought I would get on Granny's nerves. But Granny said, "Come in, baby, and sit down on the side of the bed."

Then my Cherokee great-grandmother caught my attention. I recognized her from an old photo of Mom's. She was medium in stature and had long black braids and high cheekbones. "Come over here and join us at the table," she said. My mother had spoken to me often about her Cherokee grandmother, who was a medicine woman held in high regard by the Cherokee.

Then a man I did not recognize, wearing a white robe, waved me over to the stairway. We walked upward for a short time. I then saw a beautiful, majestic view of what I knew to be the gates of heaven.

To the left side of the gates, I noticed three huge white marble seats connected to one another, the center one higher than the other two. There was a man sitting in the right-hand seat. I knew he had to be Jesus.

Beside him was God the Father. I tried to look at his face, but he was so bright, his face was a blur. He had shoulder-length, glowing white hair and beard.

When I reached the step beside them, next to the empty throne, the Father said, "Sit down here beside me, and let's talk." I sat down on what I thought would be a hard surface, but it was as soft as an overstuffed pillow.

God said, in a deep, commanding voice, "I know this all may be strange to you, but I'm glad you are here with us. And we have some decisions that need to be made."

Jesus then spoke to me in a soft, tender, loving voice, which reassured me and filled me with peace. I told him how much I needed to be with my family. "I still have some things I want to do there, like help Linda take care of the children. I don't want to leave Linda and the kids."

God said, "So it shall be." I woke up and realized the whole experience had been just an hour.

The next morning I looked in a mirror. My hair had turned from black to salt-and-pepper grey. The whole experience was real, and my hair change was a physical sign of that. Later medical tests showed I had had a heart attack.

Linda, my cousin Robert's wife, recounts:

I received a call from my husband, as usual, but this one was different from any other. Robert's voice was shaky, and I could tell he was anxious about something.

"Linda," he said, "I believe I died last night and stood in the presence of God and was given a chance to stay or leave. I know something happened to me because my hair changed color. I can't wait to get home so you can see it!"

I was convinced Robert's experience was real. I think his hair color changed because he had stood in the presence of God. I thought of Moses as he stood in that presence.

Jesus has power over life and death and is in the saving business. He rose from the grave to sit at the right hand of the Father, to make intercession on our behalf.

We have the choice to ask him into our lives, to be in fellowship with him, to follow him to heavenly heights into eternal life.

"I Found a Profound Peace and Consolation"

John Cobis, a retired Catholic high school principal, tells his story:

> 2022 is a year that will always stand out to me as one filled with sadness, confusion, and woe. Over those twelve months, more than a dozen friends and relatives passed away; the year was capped off when the first of my siblings, my sister Barbara, died on Christmas Eve. We were only a year apart in age, lived within a mile of each other, and co-owned a number of rental properties and Airbnbs.
>
> Approximately a year after the birth of her first grandchild, Barbara was diagnosed with a virulent form of cancer. Four months later she was gone. Although the Catholic faith that Barbara and I shared offered me hope and understanding, in my heart I was disconsolate and adrift spiritually.
>
> At the time I was pursuing a master's in Christian spirituality at Creighton University, as well as a certificate in spiritual direction. Creighton is a Jesuit university, so the approach to spiritual growth and discernment is based largely on the Spiritual Exercises of St. Ignatius of Loyola, the founder of the Jesuits. One of the cornerstones of Ignatian spirituality is that God communicates with us in many ways daily, and we should strive to find God in all things. As a result of this training, I became more sensitive to his presence and learned to experience him in novel ways.

I am not one who usually remembers dreams, and if I do, the memory is only a snippet, like recalling one frame from a much longer movie. I also cannot recall ever having a dream that had a lasting effect on me. But it was through a dream that the Holy Spirit gifted me with the consolation I needed regarding Barbara's death.

Barbara spent her entire career as an occupational therapist working with disabled children. She was renowned for her creativity, compassion, patience, and humor when ministering to her students. In my dream, I saw Barbara in a bright, spacious, Montessori-type classroom with many small children engaged in various individual and group activities. They were all healthy and whole and enjoying themselves. Barbara also looked healthy and joyful as various children approached her with their project for a private show-and-tell.

Barbara never acknowledged my presence, although I was standing only a few feet from her. As she spoke to each child, I could hear her refer to them as "darling," which was a favorite moniker of hers for any small child she encountered in school or out.

When I awoke from the dream, I felt a profound peace and consolation. In fact, this experience moved me so much that I shared it with my other siblings, who also appreciated the message that Barbara was well and at peace.

A Message from Grandmother (by Deacon Robert Herrmann)

I grew up in a military family. We were often on the move when I was a child. Friendships came and went, and seeing extended family was difficult and rare, especially after my father deployed to Vietnam in early 1966. However, I did have the privilege of being with my father's parents and siblings enough to create a lasting, loving impression. I had some firsthand experiences of what it meant to be a part of an extended family.

My parents met in Augsburg, Germany, in the late fifties. Dad was stationed there in the army, and my mother was working in a delicatessen. They married in Germany, but my father rotated back to California, and my mother soon followed. I never met my mother's large extended family. I had to meet them another way—through some wonderful and rich stories my mother told me.

My mother described her life in a thirteen-sibling home rich with religious, family, and cultural traditions. In many ways, how she lived her life and raised us kids—with immense fortitude, dedication, and love—was the best storytelling.

One story involved a ritual her family performed once a year. They would all walk to the family plot in the local cemetery, join hands in a circle, and pray together around their deceased loved ones. When they were finished, they would take boughs of cedar and dip them in holy water, then sprinkle the graves and ground in blessing.

Another tale came from when my mother was grammar-school age. The Allies were firebombing Augsburg, and her neighborhood was on fire. There was real fear that everything, including their home, could go up in flames.

The family gathered their rosaries and baptismal candles and began to pray. Sometime during their prayer, the flames that had drawn near the home went out. The family considered it a miraculous gift from God.

By the way, the family never blamed the Allies for the war. They knew who was responsible and despised him.

One more story from my mother's childhood: the Hitler Youth came to their front door to recruit my uncles Carl and Robert. My grandmother, standing all of five feet and two inches on a good day, stated with great sternness, "Hitler will never have my sons."

This and many other stories gave me a sense of my grandmother Anna and her character.

In my early twenties, I began traveling and helping lead parish retreats with Deacon Eddie. One week we were in beautiful Lancaster, Pennsylvania. The retreat was going well, and many people were coming out each night and bringing friends. Some even brought their Mennonite friends.

One afternoon I was praying and resting in the backyard of the host family with whom I was staying. It was a warm fall day with a clear blue sky. At one point in my prayer, I began to feel extremely homesick, especially for my mother. As I lay there, absorbed in my emotions of separation, my thoughts were carried to another memory.

I realized that I was now about the same age as my mother was when she lost her mother. They were separated by an ocean, and my mother had to grieve almost entirely on her own. This gave me compassion for my mother. My homesick feeling turned into grief for the pain she must have gone through.

Then I sensed a presence. I sensed Anna, the grandmother I'd never met. I knew as well as I knew the sun was shining that Anna was there. She came to soothe, to comfort, and to say, "It is okay for you to miss your mother. You will be okay, and what you're doing with your life is right and good."

The tears were good, but the sense of knowing that I indeed was connected to someone I'd not met in the flesh, someone so important to my formation who likely had some effect on my life choices, was quite overwhelming. Gratitude was the thing I felt most then and now, and I know I will cherish the memory of Anna's presence until one day I am able to see her face-to-face.

Chapter 7

A Messenger of Love

By Deacon Robert Herrmann

The saints we have contact with and who become instruments of God's healing are not always in heaven. Many are alive right now. Dr. Susan Sendelbach, a Catholic chaplain and psychotherapist, may be one of those saints. She shared the following story:

> In 1987, one of my first patients was a young man with AIDS named Brad. What I enjoyed most about my relationship with Brad was his incredible eagerness to know everything he could about God before he died. His search for forgiveness—which he found abundantly, shown by the depth of his repentance—warmed my heart.
>
> Brad was very excited about his spiritual growth. His questions were endless. When we would talk and pray, Brad would enter into a profound state of joy. His energy level would increase. He wanted to cram a lifetime of religious education into a few months.
>
> Sometimes his questions were about God's love or the Bible. Sometimes he asked very complex questions, as when he wanted to understand the Trinity and seemed frustrated that I couldn't help him understand it in one visit.

One funny time was when he learned that Jesus was Jewish. He looked at his mother in amazement, and said, "Why didn't you ever tell me this?" She looked equally surprised that he found this fact so astounding and responded that she thought he knew.

Brad said, "Well, if Jesus was Jewish, and I want to be as much like Jesus as possible, then I need to learn everything I can about Judaism. Maybe that's why I've been eating a lot of kosher pickles lately."

I laughed, but I so admired Brad's childlike, simple faith. He was incredibly open and determined to learn all that he could. For the next week, he insisted that dietary send him only kosher foods.

Brad trusted me. He was able to ask religious questions of me in his eager search for closeness with God. Though his body grew weaker, I saw him grow in happiness each day. We were able to laugh and joke together. He knew that I loved him and saw in him a precious child of God. I helped minister to him through religious education as well as by being a symbolic, loving presence of Jesus.

Another important discussion was when Brad wanted to know what happens after we die. I told him that no one was sure—because those who have died aren't here to tell us about it—but that we do know from the Bible and from our faith history that God is loving and forgiving. We discussed Jesus' words about eternal life.

I also told Brad that there are people who have been through an afterlife experience, having been pronounced clinically dead but then revived. He listened to the stories of near-death experiences, from books, and from stories people have shared with me. Brad seemed to draw comfort from these stories. We agreed that no one knows for sure what these afterlife experiences mean but that it would be wonderful if the light, the gardens, and the people we have known and loved are there to welcome us into the next life.

A Messenger of Love

Brad told me that if dying was like this for him, he would try to find a way to let me know. He also agreed to be one of the people to come back later to help me into the next life when it is my time to die. We hugged each other long and close, and I told him how very special he was to me.

Brad accepted the witness of my faith with total openness. Because of my constant presence with him as his chaplain, he believed that all I said to him was the truth. Each time we hugged, he would relax in my arms like a peaceful child. Stress seemed to move out of him, and smiles came across his face whenever we touched.

Brad's AIDS continued to spread to internal organs. When it reached his lungs, he was constantly on oxygen. Several times we thought that he was dying, but as with other young patients, his body was still strong and he struggled on. He continued to want prayer, support, and hugs and to ask his endless innocent questions of faith.

Brad died early one morning with his parents by his side. I was not on duty, but another one of our chaplains called to tell me.

My grief was deep. One side of me didn't want to meet the next patient with AIDS, as I felt I was hurting too much. The other half of me knew that this next person might present another special ministerial relationship.

But first I had to be with my grief. The staff that I talked with at the hospital agreed that it is difficult to lose a patient whom we love. I needed to hear more than that, but that was special beyond words.

In September, Brad's parents returned to St. Joseph's Hospital for a memorial service. They live over a hundred miles away, and they told me that they came hoping to see me. His parents said that my ministry had given them strength during the illness and loss of their son.

They wanted me to know what happened when Brad died. He had been struggling to breathe all day and night and had not talked much. He was alert to everyone around him, which is what he had hoped for, and would greet each person who came into the room by name and with a smile.

Just before his last breath, Brad reached up with his hands in the air, as if to touch something. A radiant smile came over his face, and he said to them, "Susan said there would be a bright light." And then he died.

May we all be God's messengers to the world.

CHAPTER 8

LEAD, KINDLY LIGHT

Deacon Eddie Ensley

Light imagery permeates Christian writing and prayer. References to light fill the Scriptures, particularly the Psalms: "Your word is a lamp for my feet/ and a light for my path" (NRSVCE).

The shekinah presence of the Lord guarded the children of Israel in their exodus from Egypt (Exodus 13:21-22). In the New Testament, light surrounded Jesus on Mount Tabor (Matthew 17:2). Light poured down on Paul at his conversion (Acts 9:3). Second Corinthians 3:18 says that we behold the splendor of God shining on the face of Jesus.

Throughout the Christian centuries, light metaphors and the actual experience of "inner light" have been a basic part of Christian spiritual teaching. The Anglican poet Henry Vaughan writes in his poem "The World,"

I saw Eternity the other night,
Like a great ring of pure and endless light,
All calm, as it was bright.

Jakob Bohme, a German spiritual writer of the seventeenth century, speaks of "inward light," "God's Light in the Soul," and "the Light of the Majesty." Evelyn Underhill, in her classic book *Mysticism*, documents light in the prayer experiences of the great Christian saints, calling this inward light "that light whose smile kindles the Universe."[19]

Light in the Stories of St. Francis

The stories of Francis and his early followers are full of descriptions of heavenly light. Bonaventure recounted one heart-stirring experience, when some of Francis' followers were in a boat:

> Despairing of their lives, thinking they would soon be dead, they called upon Saint Francis in suppliant fashion, a great light appeared in the boat, and with that light a calm from heaven was granted them, as if the holy man could by his wondrous power command the winds and the sea.[20]

John, an early follower of Francis, had a vision of Christ walking with him:

> Then Brother John followed him with great fervour, and when he came up to him, Christ, the blessed one, turned round, and looking at him most sweetly, he opened his holy and merciful arms and embraced him; and when he opened his arms Brother John saw rays of light come from his holy bosom, which lighted up all the forest, as well as his own soul and body. Then Brother John knelt down at the feet of Christ, the blessed one, who, as he had given his foot to Mary Magdalene to kiss, so now gave he it to Brother John. Then Brother John, taking it with great reverence, bathed it with his tears like another Magdalene.[21]

The Heavenly Light in Near-Death Experiences

A vision of great light is often a component of near-death experiences. That encounter with the powerful light of God can not only bring healing to the one who experiences it but also flow through from that person to impact people to whom they minister in their daily lives

When I was fourteen, I met Margaret Cox, a guidance counselor who impacted my life beyond measure. She was a Baptist lover of God with Catholic leanings, who always attended Easter and Christmas Catholic Masses. Heavenly light had transformed Margaret's life.

One thing almost everyone close to Margaret noticed was that she was immersed in the joy and love of God. Just by being around her, I felt God. One day she told me about her own spiritual awakening.

As a teenager, Margaret had some of the doubts a highly intellectual teenager might have. Plus, things were not always peaceful in her home.

One day, while taking a sunbath at a nearby stream, she decided to step into the water. The mud she was standing in gave way, pushing her into a part of the stream that was over her head. She later recounted to me,

> Losing my ability to stay afloat, shock and panic fill my body and mind. My arms and legs flailed in a desperate attempt to stay afloat. My terror triggered an immediate adrenaline rush. Then, before losing consciousness, I called out to the loving Savior I had learned about in Baptist Sunday school. I cried out in my mind, "Jesus, save me."
>
> I found myself going blank for a moment. No longer drowning, under me I felt the dry sand and earth holding my wet body on the shore. On that cloudy day I was surrounded by a radiance of light surpassing the brightness of the sun, constant, unchanging, and eternal, conveying the presence of God. The comfort of this embrace was so immense, words fail me.
>
> The light came from the eternal and everlasting. That light calmed me and caressed me. I breathed it in until I was saturated inside and out in that loving light. I stayed still for a moment in the light.

The next thing I remember, I felt a hand take mine. There was Jesus, perceived not just with my eyes but with my very soul. He pulled me up and embraced me. His touch warmed me. I sensed the light absorbing my negative emotions. When I exhaled, I breathed out negativity. When I inhaled, I breathed in unspeakable peace

My skin grew warm as I breathed in the light. Each time I inhaled, I breathed in the light till it soaked me in a warming, healing radiance inside and out. Each time I exhaled, I breathed out negativity and fear.

Then Jesus' hands moved from embracing me to being stretched out in blessing. He asked me to do the same. In front of us was a multitude of people. Some were crying and distressed. Others bore the stark look of loneliness. Some were physically ill, in need of comfort and healing. A high percentage were teens and young people. Light flowed from our stretched-out hands, which brought the people comfort and healing.

Then Jesus told me that he had planted a deep and holy love inside me and that my mission was to share the love with a multitude that would come to me. I felt God all around and through me. I knew from then on that my life's task was to spread his love.

After that experience, Margaret studied the Bible, reading it slowly, meditating on the words, and daily opening up to God. She told me she now felt God's presence in the core of her being, a presence that never seemed to leave her.

Just by being around Margaret, I felt the presence of God. More than what she talked about was who she was: a God-saturated person who was very healing. She loved me for who I was. She helped me love not only God but myself. The light that had enveloped her in her near-death experience poured from her to me.

Over the years, Margaret Cox touched hundreds of students' lives. She experienced the light of God and let that light shine.

In Him Is Light

After an evening of leading a congregation in prayer and talks, Sandra, a nurse around sixty, came up and told me her story. Two years before, Sandra's husband, whom she so happily loved, had died instantly in a car accident. They had no children. Over the next few years, Sandra was in tumult, supposing she had nothing to live for. Her siblings and many caring friends tried to love her and get her out of the house, but to no avail; she just withdrew.

Then Sandra had heart surgery. Very close to dying, she had a near-death experience.

Sandra found herself in a wonderful place, a meadow on the farm where she grew up. She had many fond memories of her happy, loving family. It was early evening. In the dim light before darkness settled in, Jesus stood beside her.

Vibrant light flowed from Jesus all around Sandra. She felt the light ease and relax the muscles of her neck and shoulders. The healing light moved to her arms and to the muscles of her back, her chest, her stomach, her legs and feet. She rested for a few minutes in the light of the relaxing stillness.

Sandra was now holding a candle. She saw in front of her countless people, all with lit candles. She recognized many who had loved her through the years: her husband, her parents, her many friends, and patients she had nurtured and brought to an experience of God's healing presence. She could see the lighted faces of each.

The light grew larger and brighter. An orb of light now encircled everyone, joining with the holy light that surrounded Jesus. Sandra stood there a long time, experiencing supernatural love and appreciation flowing from the crowd.

When she came back to everyday awareness, Sandra realized how many people had loved her. Some were still alive and loving her now. The sacraments, especially the Eucharist, all became fresh, bright, and wondrous. Sandra became more involved with her parish and reconnected with siblings, their families, and good friends. "Healing" was the word she used to describe it all.

Healing from Sexual Abuse

Encounters with those who have left us can help cure our greatest wounds. Jonathan, a thirty-something man, stayed after a presentation to talk with me. I had told of the woman's encounter with her nine-year-old son, recounted in chapter 1 of this book. His face beamed with joy as he told his own story of such a meeting.

Jonathan was praying before the Blessed Sacrament in his church's chapel. As he sat in silence, with nothing to distract him, a sharp ache of fear and anxiety took hold. He knew where that ache came from.

After the death of his mother, when Jonathan had just turned ten, his father hired a nanny to help with his care. The twenty-one-year-old woman was kind, even warm at times. She played with Jonathan and was comforting—for a while.

Then the nanny started abusing Jonathan sexually. This continued until just before he turned thirteen, when the nanny left to get married. Jonathan remembered the acts as dirty, sickening, and sinful. He thought they were his fault and that he was a sinner bound for hell.

But as Jonathan sat before the Blessed Sacrament, the appearance of his deceased mother shining with the light of heaven renewed his soul. As those old memories of shame bubbled up, he begged God, with tears in his eyes, to forgive and heal him. Then he felt a hand take his, from an empty chair on his right. He quickly realized it was his mother holding his hand, as she had done before her death.

Jonathan saw his mother, wearing a white robe that was shining with a heavenly brightness. He surrendered to the warmth that flooded his hand, his arm, his neck, and then his whole body. He felt safe, very safe, for the first time since his mother's death.

She asked him a question: "There is something you want to tell me, isn't there? You are hurting, and it is safe for you to tell me."

Jonathan broke down, heaving with sobs. His mother embraced him and cried too. He drank in the warm nearness of God.

As he settled, his mother told him, "My dear son, you did not do wrong. The evil acts that were done to you in no way met your needs but met hers. You were pure innocence. I have to go now, but God will continue your healing, and others also can help. Tell your pastor about this, and he will walk the pathway with you."

Hesitant at first, Jonathan met with his pastor. The pastor reassured him that the abuse was not his fault and suggested seeing a Catholic psychotherapist familiar with helping those with a history of childhood abuse. The pastor also offered to provide spiritual guidance and assist him in learning different methods of prayer and service. Before Jonathan left, the pastor administered the Anointing of the Sick.

After two weeks Jonathan told his wife, and profound healing took place in their relationship. He joined a support group for those who had been abused as children. He asked for the prayers of his mother every day.

Jonathan found solace in his faith and the support of his community. The experience reminded him of the ever-present love and care that surrounds us, even when we feel most alone. His is a powerful testimony that the powerful light of Christ heals and transforms us.

Chapter 9

God Revealed

By Deacon Eddie Ensley

Stories of near-death encounters call us to open our hearts to a deeper love and a deeper wisdom. These experiences show that God's love is tender. When we hurt, he can be right there with us to take our hand and warm our heart with his care. Truly, God is nearer to us than our heartbeat and our breath.

God can also help us face our most guarded secret, our deepest pain. He can take away the heavy burden, all the shame we carry, so that we can stand free and tall. He is as compassionate with us as a father gently wiping away the tears from an infant's cheek.

God's Little Boy

I was born breech, with the umbilical cord wrapped around my neck three times. The doctor used heavy forceps to get me out. I wasn't breathing, and the doctor said just two or three seconds more and I would have been born dead.

I seemed okay but actually had a brain injury in my right cerebral hemisphere. This was not fully diagnosed until I was a young adult. I had other brain injuries later in life, including one that put me in a coma for forty-five minutes. My condition was finally diagnosed as "major neurocognitive disorder."

When I was thirteen, I came across as awkward and confused, and I was bullied at school. Though my parents dearly loved me, my mother suffered with major depression and my father from paranoid schizophrenia. One day when I was home alone, I decided to end my life.

But first I sat on the floor and listened to Beethoven's Pastoral Symphony. Suddenly I was caught up in a whirlwind. I saw a heavenly light, brighter than a million stars, that radiated love, understanding, and compassion to my very bones. I had never been loved like this before.

I felt a presence. "Who are you?" I asked. The answer came not in human words but heart-to-heart: "I am the one who holds and comforts little boys." I knew it was Jesus in that light.

I answered, "I am not a little boy. I am thirteen, a teenager."

The answer came again without words: "You are a boy, my little boy."

I felt Jesus embrace me tightly. I could see him with the eyes of my heart and some with my actual eyes. I was finally protected and cared for. Miraculous happiness and tranquility engulfed me.

I dreamed of writing books one day, but I was failing at school.

"You will write as many books as you want to, and thousands will be touched," Jesus said. Moving a hand to my chest and pressing, he communicated to me, "I plant in your heart a compassion, a love, a message that you will write books about as well as share through speaking to vast numbers. Always remember, it is me and not you. And remember to say yes to the compassion and love as your life journeys on."

Suddenly I was caught in a whirlwind again and then was back in my room.

Wonderful things followed. When I was in high school, my parents' mental health improved. Margaret Cox, the guidance counselor whose story

I shared earlier, trained me in speaking, and I won a regional and then a state-wide oratorical contest. My grades turned to A's and B's.

I now have nineteen books published by major publishers, and have given sermons to thousands. All that Jesus had told me through the light came true.

Jimmy's Encounter with Christ

Jimmy, a young man in his early thirties, came to talk with me after Deacon Robert and I finished the last talk of a parish weekend retreat. His wife and several small children had graciously stayed home, in order to let him experience the retreat without distraction.

From the profoundly relaxed and glowing look on his face, I knew God had sunk deeply within Jimmy. As he spoke, I found out why that was so. Like many others who had talked with me on other missions and retreats, God had amazed him with his presence when he was a child. And in his case, it was through a near-death experience.

Jimmy's parents, raised Catholic, abandoned the Church before he was born. At the insistence of his maternal grandmother, a devout traditional Catholic, Jimmy was baptized at six months. His grandmother sent him to religious instruction and took him with her to church each weekend. With his parents' grudging consent, he received his First Communion when he was six.

Tragically, Jimmy's grandmother died suddenly of a stroke when he was eleven. Gone forever was this wonderful woman who expressed her love for him with hugs and warm words and told him about Jesus. Jimmy loved church, but his parents refused to take him, and though the church was just three blocks from his parents' home, they refused to let him walk there on his own. As his mother put it, "Church is just superstition. We don't want you to grow up superstitious like your grandmother."

This devastated Jimmy. He began to doubt a personal God, and that was as tragic for him as the loss of his grandmother. He wanted God to be there.

Then Jimmy suffered a concussion while playing football. To everyone's eyes he seemed dead. Yet he saw what was happening around him.

His parents came down onto the field, weeping uncontrollably. The coaches, the referees, and the ambulance team stood by, trying to get him to respond. He heard one of the coaches say his skull was cracked.

Jimmy felt himself leave his body and pass through a hall. A light as bright as the stars beckoned him to come close. The light was full of personal warmth and caring a thousand times over that of his grandmother.

Jesus was in the light, the same Jesus who was in the Host when he had received his First Communion. Jesus embraced him with warm compassion and said to him, "I have been in you all along the way. You are a special boy, and you warm my heart the same way I warm your heart. Follow me, and wonderful things will come your way." Jimmy then saw his grandmother beside him.

Jimmy was rushed to the hospital, where a surgeon operated on his head. After three weeks, he went home, and within a couple months he was very well and alive. He mustered up the courage to tell his parents about meeting God: "There is a personal God. He is in me, and I want to go back to church."

To Jimmy's surprise, his parents, with tears in their eyes, said, "We know it was real. Yes, you can go to church, and we will go with you."

"Her Pained Face Turned Soft and Radiant"

One older teenager, Jeff, attended a parish mission that Deacon Robert led. His mother had died two months earlier, and his father, Walt, had died when Jeff was four. His mother raised Jeff and his two sisters, now in their mid-twenties, alone.

Jeff described his mother as one of the most tender women he had ever known. "She helped me feel good about my life, affirming me from the depths of her, even when my behavior was a problem." Speaking as someone beyond his years in understanding, he added, "My mother now inhabits my heart." His eyes teared up.

The day before her death, the family had gathered in her hospital room. Witnessing his mother struggle with the end stage of cancer, Jeff felt as if he were coming to the end of his own life. His relatives' tight faces and tears showed that they shared his emotions.

Unexpectedly, his mother's pained face turned soft and radiant. She lifted her arms, as though beckoning someone to come close. She called out, "Walt, I am coming."

Jeff asked his mother what she had seen. She replied, "Your father and an angel surrounded by light." She fell into a coma and died the next day.

God shows his love through such encounters. Not everyone has this type of life-changing experience. We write of them because God wants all of us to know how much he cares for each and every one of us.

Chapter 10

Finding Our True Home

by Deacon Robert Herrmann

Just before my seventeenth birthday, my life seemed to be crashing in on me from every direction. Although my father had returned from Vietnam and Thailand, I still held the stress and fear in my heart of losing him to a place on the other side of the world. Though I masked it well, the stress prevented me from living fully.

My grades were less than good, I had no prayer life, and I didn't attend church. I saw my friends advancing to college and careers and myself going nowhere, without purpose or direction. Most difficult of all, there was no person I could confide in or trust with my inner life.

One night I lay in bed in total despair, feeling as though my body were in a vice. I did not feel suicidal, but I did not see any reason for living. The thing missing in my life was hope of any kind.

I felt inspired to pray. I did not know where to begin, but then I remembered how, for years, my siblings and I would pray by our bedside at night with my mother. I even prayed alone as I grew older. Somehow I'd gotten away from it.

Now I struggled to remember and reconnect. The Our Father was the only prayer I could think of, but even with that, I did not remember all the words. Slowly they came back to me, and I began to pray the Our Father over and over again.

At some point the words faded, and I felt a powerful lightness come over me. I knew I was not floating, but the sensation of utter lightness was real. It was as though I were lifted to the ceiling. There came a love, a presence beyond words, and then an engulfing warmth. Tears of pain, sorrow, and loss began to flow until my pillow was soaked on both sides of my face.

Gradually the tears changed: they were filled with an overwhelming sense of mercy streaming into me. Emptiness was being filled. There came a brightness in my heart that seemed to burst in and fill my darkened bedroom. Most dear to my memory of this experience is that I did not try to analyze it. I simply floated in the love, the warmth and beauty of this inexplicable grace.

The next day, all the same issues of the day before remained, but my vision had made a 180-degree turn. I was facing not darkness and despair but an inexplicable hope and faith that life was going to work out, and I would be okay.

I was still the same kid I had been the day before: I loved girls, fast cars, and pizza joints. But there was a new dimension to life, one that needed to be fed something other than the values I knew. I had a hunger for simplicity and clarity. I started going to church, joined an outreach group, and made friends with two Mercy nuns who helped me immensely, Sr. Amalia and Sr. Alice.

In short, this experience led me to seek fulfilment somewhere besides the trappings of secular life. Grace kept hitting me in the face until I found a way to plumb its depths through prayer. Prayer turned me outward and toward loving people, serving God and his Church through giving retreats and parish missions.

When I was only twenty years old, Cardinal Manning, the archbishop of Los Angeles, and the director of spirituality for the archdiocese, Fr. Ralph

Tichenor, SJ, heard a recording on my prayer life and invited me to Los Angeles to tell a large gathering of priests and religious sisters and brothers about prayer. Eventually I was ordained a permanent deacon in the diocese of Savannah. I continue to preach retreats on spirituality and prayer throughout North America.

God can touch us with his indescribable love and turn our lives around. I know it!

My Friend George

I first met George at a Catholic prayer group at my home parish of St. Anne. We became good friends and found that we enjoyed many of the same activities outside of church. We would often get in his VW van, which he affectionately named Rebecca, and seek out some state park to hike in or go to one of the local rivers to swim and picnic. Our favorite pastime was throwing a Frisbee up and down a large field in Lake Bottom Park. We would also take time to meditate and pray together and talk about spirituality.

After a couple years, George and I drifted apart, mostly because our lives called us in different directions. I went on to begin a lay ministry that involved a lot of travel around North America, conducting missions and retreats with Deacon Eddie. I lost touch with George and many of my local friends.

About ten years later, our local paper did a story about a man who had contracted what was then a dreaded and strange virus known as AIDS. The paper hid his identity as well as they could, but I realized that it was my old friend from the prayer group, George.

Not a lot was yet known about AIDS, except that it mostly affected men and that there was no cure; it was, simply put, a death sentence. I was overwhelmed with sadness and pity to think that my dear, kind friend had been stricken by this horrible illness. The next day, Eddie and I called George and confirmed that he was the person featured in the story.

Right off I felt God calling me to reconnect with George and try to be a friend to him for whatever days he had left. He lived for about four more years, mostly healthy at first but painfully ill in the last year.

George was married and had three beautiful children. Fortunately, all of them tested negative for the disease. George was a good and doting father.

Over time I came to find out that in the old days when I knew George, a decade earlier, when he seemed so normal and happy, were anything but. An adopted child in a large family, at the age of twelve he had been singled out by his father for depraved sexual abuse. This man held powerful emotional sway over George into his teen and young adult years.

I took time to get to know George again and enter into the pain he was still suffering. His nearness to God was intact, and his spirit was amazingly joyful and hopeful despite his illness and the loss that awaited him.

There was one thing that George wanted most before he died, and he pursued it with a level of courage I have rarely witnessed in one who had been so gravely wronged. He desperately wanted to be reconciled with his father. But the man was not interested. He refused to acknowledge any wrongdoing, going so far as to blame George for the abuse. Still George tried to reconcile.

In his last days, George often suffered terrible bodily indignities and pain. He was withered to the bones. His young son would love his father by massaging his back and staying with him for hours. Everyone knew the end was near.

One night I received a frantic call from George's wife, letting us know we should come as quickly as possible. When Deacon Eddie and I arrived, George was unconscious with a raging fever. Many of his friends and family were gathered around the bed. We stood watch and prayed and tried to comfort each other.

We all touched George and tried to convey in words our love for him. Then, while his wife was putting a cool cloth on his head, he breathed his last, quietly, peacefully, with no struggle. As his wife held him and wept over him, we stood in a circle, some holding hands and grieving.

"Thank You"

Within a minute after George passed, I felt myself embraced by a warm love that caused my body to shudder. It wasn't an emotion so much as a spiritual embrace, a communion without words pouring through my body. My spirit knew that George had passed through or around me to say, "Thank you for loving me. I love you." It was he in spirit as real as I had known him in life. I sensed George saying other things to me too. Most important for me was "Thank you for being there with me; you did so much, don't think that you didn't do enough."

I welcomed the comfort of knowing that I did not fail in my friendship with George. In my own mind, I had not done as much as I would have liked to do, and I felt guilty about that. George's words put most of that doubt to rest.

What I learned from George is that what we do for others in the name of Christ matters more than we can imagine. It matters into eternity for the one I help and hopefully for me too. Truly sacrifice is its own reward.

We Catholics have a strong belief in life after death and in the communion of saints, the ongoing connection between the Church on earth, the Church in purgatory, and the Church in heaven. The connection is real; with George it seemed barely beyond my touch.

That moment of George's death often comes back to me, and it builds my sense of closeness to Jesus and the Father. It reminds me that heaven is our true home. All that we do during this life is preparation for eternal life with God and his saints.

CHAPTER 11

How Near-Death Experiences Transform Lives

By Deacon Eddie Ensley

Near-death experiences can profoundly transform individuals who have them, as well as those who hear about them or read about them. These changes can last decades. I have heard of marriages healed as well as young people returning to the sacraments, with some going into religious life.

Catholics who have near-death experiences want to draw closer to the Church. If they have been away from the sacraments, they return. They find that the Eucharist is a way to allow the God of endless love they met near death to embrace them

"My Life Changed"

Janice, a schoolteacher, told me about her near-death experience ten years earlier. Like most who have these experiences, she stated, "My life changed." I asked her what had changed. Janice valiantly answered,

> I experienced love, love, infinite love, the love of God above all. Then I felt the love of those who have gone before, the saints and

the angels, and the love of the people now in my life. I became more spiritual, compassionate, caring, noble, and detached from material possessions, power, prestige, fame, and competition. Relations that were strained before were restored to peace and compassion.

When I was in my twenties, I had to divorce my first husband. He had been violently abusive and controlling to the point that it was not safe to stay.

I had been known as a calm person with a healing personality. People came to me with their problems, and I had the wisdom to help them. But after the traumatic time with my husband, I needed healing myself.

After several years, I fell in love with another lapsed Catholic, a man who had lost his wife to an accident years before. It ended up being a mutually good relationship, a sustaining relationship. But I could not go to Communion if I was honest with myself and God.

I didn't know what to do. That man's love was so important to me. We got along well, and we learned how to fight and reconcile beautifully and love one another in moving ways. I married him outside the Church, since my first marriage was not annulled.

Then I had a heart attack. I sensed myself being carried through a tunnel toward a beautiful orb of light. That light was love. That love filled my nostrils. That love touched every cell of my body with the realization that God loves me.

God gave me a message, not in human words but in a silence too deep for words: "Draw near the sacraments and the Church." God was showing me his presence in that love surrounding me.

Several weeks later, I got a good bill of health. I wanted that love that had touched me. I knew I could find it in people, in caring for others. And I could find it in prayer. I knew I had to go back to Mass, even though I could not receive the Eucharist

I wanted to be in the Church. I prayed and worked up the courage to talk with my pastor. He said, "Think about getting an annulment. It may well be that your first husband never had the right intentions in marrying you, and he was wrong in making that decision at that time. Most people find an annulment to be something that heals."

Janice agreed, though she was scared of what it would mean. She had to go over things in her first marriage and in herself that were hard to look at. With the courage of Jesus' love, she was able to do that, letting go of negativity and forgiving. She found the process curative. The marriage was annulled, and Janice was free to marry in the Church, a great joy for her.

The healing Janice experienced helped her forgive others who had hurt her. She experienced a strong impetus to bring healing to people who came to her with their hurts. She joined a prayer group especially for praying for people who needed healing. It was heartwarming to touch people who had those hurts and help them forgive, help them find love, and help them find healing through God's most gracious gift of mercy.

"Reconsider Your Life"

A young man I'll call Peter, around thirty-five, told me of his near-death experience when he was just seventeen. At the time, he enjoyed people at his high school, and they enjoyed him. Some said he was the most popular boy in the school.

But Peter was having a hard time deciding what profession to pursue. His grades were not the best, and so he would have to go to a local community college. He wasn't looking forward to the struggle of finding a good academic path.

Peter also found it hard to maintain romantic relationships. He enjoyed them but was always ready to move on to the next best thing. His priority of having fun and doing what suited him prevented him from having a meaningful relationship with anyone. He hurt a lot of young women.

Peter had an accident in his home. He fell down some steps and broke his ribs, puncturing his arms. He stopped breathing and was near death.

During that time, Peter said, he could see everything around him. He saw his sister hysterically crying for help. He saw policemen and the emergency technicians working on him, trying to bring back a heartbeat. He saw it all clearly.

Then he saw below him what seemed like hell: people being tortured by their own sinfulness, people without the presence of God, rejecting God. It scared him so much that he did something he had not done in years: he prayed. "Dear God, I can't handle this myself. Help me, Lord. Rescue me."

A ball of light came over him. He breathed it in. He felt it release him from his fears.

Peter heard a voice: "You have many good friends. Think of their love for you. But you are living for yourself only. You are trying to avoid the consequences of your actions. Your future depends on your openness to God and his helping you embrace and love those who need to be embraced and loved. The goodness that you grew up in can become a healing force for many. Reconsider your life."

These were powerful words. Peter felt the presence of God in the light, warming and healing him. God felt as near to him as his own breathing. He knew not only that he was loved but that he needed to love others and to tell them about that love. The Lord said—without words, in the tender voice of God's silence—"Reconsider what you do with your life. You have so much to give." Then, "It is time to go back to your body."

A month of constant care brought Peter back to normal life. The love he felt from God was so much greater than the love he had felt from being popular at school. He wanted to do something meaningful with his life.

Peter felt drawn to the Church, which he had stopped attending when he was fifteen. The sacraments heightened his experience of God's love. He made friends with students who were bullied, students who were unpopular. His presence in their lives helped them feel loved and gave them confidence.

Still there were academic decisions to make. Priesthood seemed an obvious way to give to others. He might have to go to community college before the seminary would consider him, due to his poor grades. His senior year, he worked his best to get his grades up and hoped that would be enough.

Then Peter thought about how he liked dating. He wanted love and enjoyed being with the young women in his school. "The priesthood would be great," he decided, "but I'm not built for it."

Peter decided to try nursing. He would be able to help people and still date, fall in love, and get married—if that was God's plan for him.

The Church became a great sustenance for Peter; the love he found there enveloped him. The people, the pastor, the priests, and the lay workers showed him, by their presence and their prayers, what it meant to be open to God. He joined the young adult group and played a vital role in designing retreats and being a mentor to the younger guys. Some seemed surprised that a popular athlete would take time to be with them.

Peter worked hard to get good grades in nursing school, and he excelled in caring for people. He met a beautiful young woman, also studying to be a nurse, whom he dated and married.

As a nurse in a Catholic hospital, from time to time Peter has had occasion to speak about his near-death experience, helping people who are grieving and those who are seriously ill. Several people in his care also had near-death encounters, and Peter helped them realize that it was something good in God's hands.

CHAPTER 12

WHAT ABOUT PURGATORY AND HELL?

By Deacon Eddie Ensley

While most people who have near-death experiences have a positive encounter with light and love, some get a glimpse of what they believe to be hell.

The Church teaches that God's mercy is boundless, and his deep wish is the salvation of all souls. She urges believers to embrace grace and avoid the path leading to eternal separation from God. As Pope Francis stated, "Our infinite sadness can only be cured by an infinite love."[22]

Heaven is the state of supreme happiness where souls enjoy perfect life with the Holy Trinity, the Virgin Mary, angels, and all the blessed. Hell, on the other hand, is excluding oneself from communion with God. Hell is for those who refuse to repent and accept God's mercy, even at the moment of death. The chief punishment of hell is eternal separation from God, in whom alone a person can experience the life and happiness for which they were fashioned. Contemplating hell encourages us to center ourselves on the Love that contains all other loves, God himself.

Purgatory, on the other hand, is a temporary purification state for those who have died in God's grace but still need cleansing. It is not punishment but mercy, preparing souls for heaven. The faithful can help these souls through prayers, Masses, and almsgiving.

Individuals who have unpleasant encounters with what they believe to be hell are often transformed as a result. They usually describe this experience as a deep, frightening darkness without God, where they fear they will spend eternity. They call on God for help.

Such people often realize this as a second chance at life, a time to discover God and to change in the ways God wants them to change. Most of the people I have heard speak about seeing hell tell of God rescuing them.

Encountering the Darkness

As Dr. Bruce Greyson and Nancy Evans Bush put it in an article for *Missouri Medicine*:

> A classic response to profound spiritual experience is conversion, not necessarily changing one's religion but in the original sense of the Latin *convertere* meaning "to turn around." The terrifying NDE is interpreted as a warning about unwise or wrong behaviors and a sign to turn one's life around: "I was being shown that I had to shape up or ship out, one or the other. In other words, 'get your act together,' and I did just that."

In the same article, clinical social worker Kimberly Clark Sharp observes,

> All the people I know who have had negative experiences have become Bible-based Christians.... They might express it in various sects. But they all feel that they have come back from an awful situation and have a second chance.[23]

Such experiences are recorded not only in modern near-death experiences. Venerable Bede tells the story of a married Northumbrian man, Drithelm, who fell sick with a fever for several days. He died but then came back to life.

When he returned, he comforted his mourning wife, "Fear not, for I am now truly risen from death, and permitted again to live among men; however, I am not to live hereafter as wanted."

Drithelm experienced the light of heaven but was also shown the dark pit of the absence of God, which he believed to be hell. He changed his life, and he prayerfully told others of his journey into light and viewing the pit of hell. He hoped to inspire people to center their lives on God and loving others.[24]

An Atheist Transformed

One of the most moving stories I have ever heard is of an atheist professor, Howard Storm, whose life was transformed after he saw images of hell and then of God. *My Descent into Death* is Storm's account of his near-death experience in Paris, his full recovery back home in the States, and the subsequent transformation of his life. Storm also communicates what he learned in his conversations with heavenly beings on the meaning of life, what happens when we die, the role of angels, and much more. His account will challenge those who believe that human awareness ends with death.

For many years, Howard Storm enjoyed the accomplishments of the American dream, with a fine home, a family, and a successful career as an art professor and painter. Unexpectedly, he found himself in a hospital enduring severe pain, awaiting emergency surgery. Confronted with the possibility of death, Storm believed that his passing would signify the end of consciousness. As he put it, "My whole life had been one of self-sufficient stoicism. I believed I didn't need anyone's help. I could handle anything. I could do this, I thought."[25]

What transpired was not what Storm expected. He experienced an out-of-body state, observing his physical form from an external perspective. This was not a mere hallucination; he felt more conscious and alive than ever. In his spiritual form, Storm was propelled into ominous realms of darkness, where he confronted the consequences of a life of selfishness and materialism.

Storm heard a voice say, "Pray to God." He thought this just added to his helplessness. He had no idea how to pray.

A second time the voice spoke to him: "Pray to God." It was recognizably his own voice deep within him, but he had not spoken. He did not have the slightest concept of how to pray. His lips had not moved in prayer since childhood. He was sure he couldn't pray. He wouldn't know what to say!

The voice within him said once more, "Pray to God!" The voice was urgent. Storm was unsure what to do.

> Praying, for me as a child, had been something I had watched adults doing. It was something fancy and had to be done just so. I tried to remember prayers from my childhood experiences in Sunday school. Prayer was something you memorized. What could I remember from so long ago? Tentatively, I murmured a few lines—a jumble from the Twenty-third Psalm, "The Star-Spangled Banner," the Lord's Prayer, the Pledge of Allegiance, "God Bless America," and whatever other churchy sounding phrases came to mind. "Yea, though I walk in the valley of the shadow of death, I will fear no evil, for thou art with me. For purple mountain majesty, mine eyes have seen the glory of the coming of the Lord. Deliver us from evil. One nation under God. God Bless America.[26]

Then a very old tune from Storm's childhood started going through his head. It sounded like a little boy singing the same line over and over again. The child that he had once been was singing, full of innocence, trust, and hope. "Jesus loves me, da da da . . ." He and his classmates had sung that song.

Right away an enormous, loving light engulfed Storm. This was a living being, a luminous being approximately eight feet tall and surrounded by an oval of radiance. In that light was Jesus, who hugged him with an embrace that contained an eternity of love.

Storm's journey continued to luminous regions, where he communicated with angelic beings and a supreme entity referred to as the Lord of Light. These instructed him to return to earthly life with a message centered on love.

After this experience, Storm began a process of reconciling his life with what he had learned while out of his body. He visited Gethsemane Cistercian Abbey, where he was especially touched at the grave of Thomas Merton. He eventually gave up teaching art and is currently serving as a pastor.

My Descent into Dearth is raw, unfiltered, and powerful, dealing with suffering and change. Storm's open questioning of his experience suggests intellectual authenticity and beauty. He approaches traditional Christian ideas realistically and uses modern language to describe them.

Storm's experience reminds us to center our lives on God, to wrap our imaginations and our thoughts around him. This is true prayer of the heart. Such prayer can reside in our inner depths, where our identity and behavior are influenced.

Messages like those Storm heard from Jesus counteract the negative messages we may receive from others. We can stop lying to ourselves and begin to access the deeper levels of truth that result from preparing our souls for our intimate meeting with God.

"Father, Please Forgive Me"

Lois, a middle-aged teacher, received what she thought was a vision of hell during her near-death experience. She went through a tunnel, a place of frightening darkness, without God. She heard screams and fiercely angry voices swearing at one another.

Lois was terrified that she might be in that place forever. Scenes from her life passed through her mind. She had not taken care of her husband during his terminal illness but left his care to his elderly mother and two brothers. She let snippets of anger and inconvenience come out when she was near him.

Lois also had secret liaisons with her husband's cousin. She was now having an affair with a married teacher, and his attention toward her was ruining his formerly solid marriage.

Lois now felt all the pain she had caused. She realized that she did not know how to express true love to anyone. She felt herself drowning in guilt.

Lois didn't feel she could ask God for help. But paraphrasing Christ's words from the cross, she cried out, "Father, please forgive me, I didn't know what I was doing."

Suddenly Lois was surrounded by an utterly loving light. She fell into Christ's embrace. Her mind went back to her childhood, when she was beaten countless times by her alcoholic parents. Jesus' arms absorbed that pain, loving her deep inside where she had never been loved before.

Lois returned to her body. She eventually healed from her illness and returned home. She immediately broke off her relationship with the male teacher. Then she picked up the phone and, though it was difficult to do, made an appointment with her pastor. She spent an hour in the Sacrament of Reconciliation, confessing a lifetime of sins and hurts.

After absolution, Lois felt as pure as a mountainside covered with snow. Her near-death experience led to a true transformation.

Praying for People

I have spoken with others who witnessed hell as part of their near-death experience. One man, Matt, loved God intently throughout his life. He came to him in the sacraments and had an open heart, reaching out to others, especially the poor.

Matt experienced overwhelming love, joy, and compassion in his near-death experience. Then three angels transported him to a place from which he saw hell and heard the screams. This was not to warn him but to give him a sense of urgency to pray for and show compassion to those who made no room in their lives for God, Scripture, or the sacraments. It also reminds us to pray fervently for those who have passed on and may be in a state of purgation.

CHAPTER 13

NEAR-DEATH EXPERIENCES ARE REAL

Skeptics contend that the near-death experience is a hallucination. Some suggest that these experiences are similar to those of someone who takes LSD. However, LSD causes distortions in reality, in terms of place and time. Near-death experience accounts come from various cultures and are "more orderly, logical, defined, and predictable than comparable accounts of drug- or illness-induced hallucination."[27]

People who have near-death experiences believe that they are real and that they greatly impact their lives. They report experiences such as floating above their bodies, going through a tunnel, meeting and embracing a loving light who certainly seems like the Judeo-Christian God. In studies of cardiac cases, a person whose heart stops can vividly and accurately remember the activity of the people around them, while their brains show no activity on the monitor. "Seventy-four percent [indicate] profound awareness of what was going on, more aware, more conscious than in everyday living."[28]

A Mother's Witness

Jacob and Martha, a brother and sister, experienced a marvel together, though Martha had settled in South Carolina and Jacob lived in Idaho.

They had grown up in an economically stretched family. Their father suffered from mental illness. The cost of health services would have been too much, and in any event, he was not willing to seek help. He was abusive to the two children. He died in a car accident when the kids were both in their early twenties.

Their mother had always shown them lots of love and tried to shield them from the father's verbal abuse. But this was not enough in the children's minds. Both schoolteachers, they could afford to visit her only every year or two.

In her eighties, the mother developed an aggressive form of stomach cancer. The doctors gave her only six months to live. Both children found the funds to visit her. Their mother told them how much she loved them and that she wished things had been better.

Martha and Jacob were at their mother's bedside on the last day of her life. Pain wracked her, and uncertainty came over her. She did not seem to know the right things to say. Yet they noticed that as she approached death, she said things like "Death is not to be dreaded. I know there is more." Both Martha and Jacob, now agnostic, doubted that.

Then their mother looked up from her bed, smiled, reached her arms out, and said, "It's angels coming to get me."

This went on for a couple days. She was talking to her own parents, saying to the children, "Your grandparents are coming to get me." Just before she died, she raised her arms, as though inviting someone in. She said, "Jesus is coming to get me."

Martha and Jacober were broken by her death. They wished that some things could have been said. They wanted to believe that she was going to a God who was real and that she actually saw angels and relatives in her dying days, though this challenged their agnosticism. Both grieved deeply as they returned to their respective homes.

Two weeks later, Jacob woke up one morning and saw his mother in the room. She took his hand, and he felt the solidity of it. She said, "I want to introduce you to Jesus. He can make things whole and new."

She waited a moment, and then a voice came through a barely open door, "I love your mother, and I love you too."

Jacob's mother said, "I wish I had listened to you when your father was hurting you and your sister. I wish I had comforted you. I wish I had had the courage to take you out of it. Please forgive me."

Jacob answered, "I forgive you, Mother."

There was now a light in the room, a lovely light, the light of God. Jacob felt an intense, incredible love. Things that had bothered him were all touched, healed by a love so vast he could not comprehend it.

Jacob eventually mustered the courage to call his sister and tell her of their mother's visit. To his surprise, Martha said, "Mother came to me the night you mentioned. And like you, she was loving me, and the light of God surrounded me. That light brought healing to my heart. That light drew me near, and it was healing within. It calmed my fears and uncertainties and healed the baggage I was carrying from my past. I knew that God was real and that he took care of us."

Both were astounded that they had visions that were almost identical. They both became active in the Church. They know that God is real and that life eternal is real.

Jacob applied for a job near Martha so that they could be together as a family. They were able to help people in need, particularly lending spiritual help to those who were grieving a loved one's death. This ministry became an occasion to assure others that the afterlife is real and that God loves with a tremendous healing presence.

An Intellectual Rediscovers God

James grew up in a stable, supportive home and was well-known for his excellence in academics. His parents were both doctors. While they attended Mass occasionally, his grandmother was the faithful Catholic who supported James in receiving his First Communion and Confirmation.

James' parents gave him the best things that they could buy but found it difficult to develop a close relationship with their only child. His grandmother's death brought an end to the warmth, care, and support he needed.

Throughout high school, James hung out with highly intelligent people who shared his love for academics. He and his friends would argue about philosophy and politics. James still defended the reality of God, but he did it without a clear feeling of God within.

James enjoyed going on dates, but he never allowed young women to really get to know him. In many ways he seemed emotionless.

While attending university, James found himself very much alone. He majored in philosophy, with the goal of becoming a philosophy professor. This angered his parents, who wanted him to go on to medical school. With his high academic abilities, they were sure he could become a great doctor. But James wasn't interested.

James would walk across campus with his head either in a book or in the clouds. One afternoon he didn't notice an oncoming car. The driver tried to stop, but it was too late.

James lay crumpled on the ground, unconscious. During the ambulance ride to the hospital, he stopped breathing and went two minutes without a pulse. He remained in a coma for a few days.

As James lay in his hospital bed, comatose, everything was clear to him. He could see the doctors working on him, and he could hear their conversations. He felt surrounded by an overwhelming sense of love, as if someone were hugging him and saying, "I have always loved you. I will be with you." It was Jesus.

James said to Jesus, "I am so lonely. I don't know how to be a person like everybody else."

Jesus embraced him and said, "I will be with you always. Trust in me as someone who will always love you."

James also saw his grandmother. She said, "I love you too, and that love will always be with you. Jesus will always be with you, and I will be with Jesus when he loves you."

James could see his past, how he had hurt people and how others had hurt him. And he saw his loneliness. He saw times when people did not reach out to him. He also saw times when people did reach out to him but he could not return their warmth and friendship—and he saw how that had hurt them.

James also saw colorful fields of flowers, more colorful than any on earth. He could smell the scents of springtime and hear the sound of rushing water. Everything reflected the God of love. He wanted to stay immersed in that love, but Jesus told him, "You must return. You will find love as you live your life. The time will come when you will return here."

James awoke, back in his body with all the pain and hurt from the accident. The doctors confirmed that his description of what they had said was accurate, even though his heart had stopped beating and the medical team thought that they had lost him.

James never forgot all that he had seen and heard while he was in that coma—and it changed him. When he went back to college, he joined a fellowship group of Catholic students. He made the effort to develop friendships with classmates who loved God. They talked about the Lord together and studied Scripture, but they also went out to movies, played video games together, and attended social events. He began to experience the love that Jesus had promised him—and it changed his life.

Even James's career plans changed. He transferred to a Catholic university, where he earned a degree in Catholic studies. Later he earned his master's degree and became a religious education director at one of the largest parishes in his diocese. He fell in love and married a wonderful woman. They welcomed children, and they now share Jesus' transforming love with them.

Chapter 14

What Are Visions and Mystical Experiences?

By Deacon Eddie Ensley

I sat in the church office of a large parish in the Midwest with six of the parish staff. Deacon Robert and I had just finished preaching a mission there. One of the things I had talked about is the wondrous, how heaven is nearer to each of us than we dare believe. I gave the staff members a chance to respond with their own stories.

One middle-aged woman, the accountant, started off. "My family has experienced the wondrous too." Reluctantly at first but with growing confidence, she told of a powerful near-death experience.

She was a little girl in a family of six children. One of the older boys was out delivering papers and was not home in time for supper. Everyone was worried. In about thirty minutes, they were going to start a search for him.

As the mother of the family mulled this over alone in her bedroom, she had a powerful sense of God's presence. With her eyes wide open, she saw the glowing figure of an angel. The angel said, "Your son has come home to be with God. He's okay, and grace will be with you."

A hard knock came at their door a few minutes later. The mother knew it was a policeman. Her son, who had been on a bike, had been hit by a car and killed. The loss was terrible but was softened by the mother's experience, which she shared with her family.

This story had previously been told only within the family. We were all amazed. Tears trickled down the accountant's cheeks: tears because God was there, along with tears of loss for her brother.

As we went around the room, each person had some wondrous story of God's work in their life. Such events do not happen just to saints or holy people in history. They happen to ordinary people like you and me.

The Prevalence of Near-Death Experiences

Rev. Ben Johnson was a Lutheran minister with a doctorate in theology from Harvard. Back in the eighties, he and sociologist Milo Brekke surveyed two thousand Christians in mainline churches in St. Cloud, Minnesota. They found that 30 percent had seen dramatic visions, heard heavenly voices, or experienced prophetic dreams.

Johnson told a joint meeting of the Society of Biblical Literature and the American Academy of Religion, "Two centuries after the intellectual world has said that these kinds of things do not happen, they show up among almost a third of the population in a conservative Midwestern city."[29]

A newer study of NDEs included participants from thirty-five countries.

> The research team recruited 1,034 people via an online crowdsourcing platform to eliminate selection bias and asked them if they had ever experienced an NDE. Those who answered yes were asked for more details using a detailed questionnaire assessment tool, the Greyson Near-Death Experience Scale, which inquires about sixteen specific symptoms.
>
> A total of 289 people reported an NDE, with 106 of those reaching a threshold of 7 on the Greyson NDE Scale, thereby

confirming a true NDE. Approximately 55 percent of them perceived the NDE as truly life-threatening.[30] They reported various spiritual and physical phenomena: abnormal time perception (87 percent), exceptional speed of thought (65 percent), exceptionally vivid senses (63 percent), and feeling separated from or out of their bodies (53 percent). Sensations included feeling at total peace, hearing angels singing, being aware of being outside the body, seeing their lives flash before them, and being in a dark tunnel before reaching a bright light.

These experiences were equally prevalent among individuals who were not in imminent danger of death as among people who were in genuinely life-threatening situations—such as heart attacks, car accidents, near drowning, and combat scenarios.

Wisdom from Pop

It can seem like an impossible task to describe visions in words because visions and near-death experiences transcend our limited language. These experiences are real and provide knowledge of God and ourselves, despite our struggle to describe them clearly. My Cherokee grandfather, whom I called Pop, was the first to teach me how to discuss visions.

Pop often talked about an incident that happened before I was born, back when my father was still in high school. Pop was working by the riverbank with some wires and was shocked by a loose one. He nearly died.

Pop saw a beautiful light surrounding him and the land on both sides of the river. Across the river, rather than woods he saw lovely trees, grass, and hills. He knew it was the land of eternity. Jesus, dressed as a Cherokee, stood beside him and embraced him, and their two hearts beat together. Jesus told Pop that he was planting a deep wisdom within him, a wisdom to share with his children and grandchildren. Then he let him return to this earth.

In his later years, Pop would spend hours roaming the woods at the top of the bluff above the river or walking on the riverbank. He would look at the rocks and plants. Often he would appear to be doing nothing, just gazing at the landscape or water.

When 1 was a young boy, I would follow Pop. I have a vivid memory of my grandfather standing motionless on the top of a bluff, letting his eyes soak in all that came to him. Once I asked him what he saw. I can still hear his answer, rhythmic with Cherokee and Appalachian intonations: "I see the dirt, the trees, the water, the skies."

"Why?" I asked him. "Why do you look so long?"

He paused, took his pipe out of his mouth, swallowed, and then slowly said, "If you look a long time, it will all shimmer, and you will see the glory."

I have no doubt that Pop saw the glory. He was telling me what a vision is. In visions and mystical experiences, life shimmers, and we see the glory. Visions are perceptions of God's splendor, the glory that knits and ties all things together.

I'm amazed at how similar Pop's language was to that of the Jewish writer Rabbi Samuel Dresner:

> God did not forsake the world after having created it. His love for His creation manifests itself in His constant effort to reach down to it. At Sinai His voice broke through the curtain which man had painstakingly erected. Never again was it heard so clearly and so decisively, but the effort on His part to speak to His creatures never ceases. Saintly souls of all ages have caught echoes of the beyond. ... This outpouring from heaven to man is called ... shefa, and may be likened to the rays which emanate from the sun, ceaselessly reaching out to brighten the darkness of the world, ... which endlessly and lovingly flows from heaven.[31]

The Connection between the Natural and Supernatural Worlds

Before the Enlightenment, miracles and visions were considered natural events that provoked wonder and awe. For theologians like St. Augustine, everything was both natural and miraculous. He saw natural phenomena—such as rain, snow, and wind—as manifestations of a greater mystery. When people became accustomed to these ordinary events, special signs were needed to remind them of the extraordinary nature of their surroundings.

Visions, including near-death experiences, can transform, heal, and brighten our lives.

In an adult education class on spiritual experiences, I showed a beautiful icon of Christ and asked if it was true or false. No hands were raised. I then played Gregorian chant and repeated the question, receiving only perplexed looks. Sacred art and music aren't judged as true or false; they guide our imaginations and emotions toward the mysterious and the holy.

Near-death visions and mystical experiences do not serve as road maps or direct orders from heaven. They possess a truth similar to that of an icon or a chant, surpassing rational thought with a quality of transcendence. The inner senses and images in these visions hold meanings beyond their basic interpretations.

Our visions are fallible, much as we are. Mystery interacts with our fallibility, producing visions when we encounter the sacred and are left without words. These visions introduce mystery into the everyday, creating meaningful metaphors and memories that can be explored throughout our lives.

Visions often serve as a means of communication with ourselves and connecting with the divine. They emerge from within as a language that aids in understanding. Sharing visions with others is a way to convey mystery. Recalling and retelling these experiences allows us to transmit this sense of mystery to others.

Like the language of our dreams, the language of visions is not one that we consciously make up or choose but a language that spontaneously emerges from our preconscious depths. Modern studies in brain physiology strongly suggest that our brains are designed for mystical experiences and visions. God, it would seem, built into our very bodies an ability to form languages of feeling, symbols, stories, and sounds that convey to us the touches and interruptions of God's grace.

Christian mystics often speak of the encounter with God as "heavenly discourse." "The Word has often come to me," St. Bernard would say of his brushes with God. The Word is a word. Jesus, the Word made flesh, comes in visions to give us words to speak and to cherish.

We can speak these words to others as well as to ourselves. They can change our speech and knit us to one another. That is how visions often function in older societies that are not so saturated with the media and cerebral abstractions. Visions are a gift of connectedness. They smash our isolation from God, one another, and all of creation, as well as from our inmost selves. Visions provide tapestries of light that connect our inner and outer worlds, that tie us together as human beings. Visions reveal insights from within.

Neuroscientists are discovering that our bodies may be built for visions. Researchers at the University of California, San Diego's brain and perception laboratory are finding compelling evidence that "the human brain may be hardwired to hear the voice of heaven." Other studies suggest that our brains respond uniquely and intensely to sacred words such as God.[32]

Social scientists report that people have visions all the time, even though the visions can't be discussed in many circles. Visionaries are found in the suburbs, not just in the pages of the Bible, among Native Americans, or in biographies of saints.

Common sense suggests that phenomena this widespread point to a widely shared human ability—in this case, the ability to perceive the sacred. Our contemporary hungering for the spiritual is an effort to recover something that human beings have always had. Human beings in the past did not seek after visions the way we do today; they didn't have to. Visions were a normal part of their lives.

Visions aim to bring holiness into everyday life, adding mystery to the ordinary and making our lives shimmer. Many have encountered mystery; it leaves us speechless, pulling us into an awe-filled and loving unknown.

CHAPTER 15

THE HOPE OF THE RESURRECTION

By Deacon Eddie Ensley

The Church grew beautifully from the experience of miracles. Preaching about this great mystery in our tradition will be part of the way this enters the Church again, so that it can open us to the marvelous ways God works in us, to show us himself, his love, and heaven.

When I give talks at retreats, I usually pick out two or three lively faces in the audience—people whose eyes light up, who closely follow what I am saying. I find such faces reassuring, and I keep my eyes on them during much of the talk, as if we were having a private conversation.

At one retreat many years ago, an elderly couple, their faces bright with joy, seemed to be drinking in every word I said. It was as if a light came from their hearts to mine and knit us together. I felt this, and I think they felt it too.

During a three-hour break, the couple took me aside and said, "We want to ask you to do something for us. We would like to take a while and talk to you about it."

Normally I would have to say no to such a request. I need those breaks to renew my energy and to go over ideas for the upcoming sessions. But I knew I needed to spend time with this couple.

Remembering a Loved Child

We found an empty classroom away from everyone else, and they began to share their lives with me. It was obvious that they were deeply in love with each other and always had been. They seemed like people who were naturally good and didn't have to try hard, as most of us do. Love naturally flowed from them. But as with most people who are able to love genuinely, suffering had played a role in their lives.

They told me about their only child, Robby, who had been born right after World War II. The little boy was the sunshine of their lives. They shared stories with me about him that were funny and touching.

When Robby was six years old, he became sick one day with what they thought was the flu. It was really meningitis, and the next day Robby was dead. Every month since his death, the couple had placed a new toy on his grave, and they kept his memory shining bright.

Age had isolated these two, as their family and most of their friends were dead. They feared both being left alone and leaving the other one alone; they had known so much caring, so much love from each other.

They looked at me and from their hearts said, "We want you to do something for us. We want you to remember. When you pray, remember us. And please remember the stories we told you about our son, because we lament that all knowledge of him will leave the earth with us. After we are gone, if you are ever in this part of the country again, if you at all can, please go by his grave and leave a toy."

Without thinking about it, the three of us formed a circle and put our hands on one another's shoulders. We stayed there for a long time with tears of grief trickling down our cheeks. Their willingness to grieve helped me grieve over some of the losses in my life. After a while, I said, "Oh, yes, I will remember. And I'll tell other people to remember."

As the tears ceased, we were enfolded in the heart of God. His heart beat with our hearts; he breathed in our breath. We felt a powerful hope, a powerful joy, an intimation of resurrection coursing through our arms to one another—a bright, astonishing hope that only God can bring. The faith we have is that our anguish will not overwhelm us, but the hurt will open us to the astonishing surprises of God.

This couple had spent thirty-five years acknowledging the hurt, and their lives flowed with the reality of their hope. My experience with them helped me cope with a profound loss that was to come into my life.

"You Will Have to Believe for Me"

In 1986 my cousin Billy Joe died suddenly and unexpectedly. He was an only child, as I am, and I had always regarded him as a brother and his parents, My Aunt Margaret and Uncle Bill, as second parents. A few weeks after his death, a car accident instantly killed Uncle Bill and left Aunt Margaret seriously injured (she fully recovered).

In my grieving, my faith made little sense for a while. I felt no comfort or hope. I was desolate. I told my friends, "You will have to believe for me."

I was powerless to hope as an act of my will. Then one day I was reading an old funeral service for children, "The Mass of the Angels." I read, "May the angels bear you upon their wings to paradise." The words resonated in the inner chamber of my heart.

Somehow I knew, with a knowing that is beyond words, that Billy and Uncle Bill rested in the bosom of Jesus. I could not have talked myself into such knowledge; it came as a gift. My whole body was filled with the white light of hope, the hope that only the Holy Spirit can bring. As theologian Walter Brueggemann once wrote, "Our hope is never generated among us but given to us. And whenever it is given we are amazed."[33]

Only God Can Bring Us Hope

We cannot produce hope in ourselves; we cannot talk ourselves into it. Hope is like the wind. We can put out our sail and make it ready to receive, but only God can bring the wind.

Real Christian hope comes only when we accept the magnitude of the loss. If we hide away the hurt, we close our hearts to hope. It's only as we embrace the pain and the loss that hope can come.

After grieving will come comfort; after a night of weeping, joy in the morning; after brokenness, mending; after hostility, forgiveness; after estrangement, reconciliation; after repression and dehumanization, justice; after death, homecoming and resurrection.

In the resurrection of Jesus Christ, the future broke into the present. Jesus fully embraced the heartache of the whole world and spoke a powerful word of newness. His coming is the rising sun that chases away all shadows, dispels all doubt, and comforts all grief.

His resurrection lights up the shadows of our hearts. It brings a love as wide as the earth, as free as the open sky, as deep as the deepest river, as gentle as the spring wind. His rising is the sun that shatters the darkness; it stills the unsettled waters within our hearts; it is the bridge that crosses the stormy sea of our pain, the medicine that cures our hurts.

The risen Lord is the calm weather after the storm; he enfolds the universe in his tender mercy. It is, as Karl Barth put it, "the glory of God investing the whole creation of every time and place with unspotted and imperishable glory."[34]

Afterword:
A Look toward the Future

Miracles have been widespread in the Catholic tradition. St. Augustine wrote at length about miracles in his church, including near-death experiences. He talked about them from the pulpit and would have those who experienced miracles speak in front of the church.

St. John Chrysostom, perhaps the greatest theologian in the Eastern Church, also spoke from the pulpit and in his personal and pastoral letters about these types of experiences. Early Franciscans were familiar with the world of near-death experiences and visions. This long history of such experiences in the Church is one of the reasons to take visions and near-death experiences seriously today. Ordinary people can share about the profoundly healing love of God reaching into their lives.

As a person of faith, I would say that our physical self was made to experience God. Our bodies and souls are missing something when we don't hear and talk about these times when God so beautifully loves us, body and soul.

Miracles occur today. Prayerfully we can help one another share them, for the glory of God!

Notes

[1] C. S. Lewis, *Mere Christianity* (The Macmillan Company, 1970), 118.

[2] "Dr. Jeffrey Long and Evidence of the Afterlife," *Life after Life*, March 15, 2021, https://www.lifeafterlife.com/blog/dr-jeffery-long-and-evidence-of-the-afterlife.

[3] Marcus Dods, *Forerunners of Dante: An Account of Some of the More Important Visions of the Unseen World, from the Earliest Times* (Edinburgh: T & T Clark, 1903), 177-79, English modernized.

[4] St. John Chrysostom, "Letter to a Young Widow," in *Nicene and Post-Nicene Fathers*, First Series, Vol. 9, ed. Philip Schaff (New York: Cosimo, 2007), 123.

[5] St. Ambrose, "Book I: On the Decease of His Brother Satyrus," in *Nicene and Post-Nicene Fathers*, Second Series, Vol. 7., eds. Philip Schaff and Henry Wace (Grand Rapids, Michigan: Wm. B. Eerdmans Publishing Company, 1955), 172.

[6] St. Gregory Nazianzen, "Oration VII: Panegyric on His Brother Caesarius," in *Nicene and Post-Nicene Fathers*, Second Series, Vol. 7., eds. Philip Schaff and Henry Wace (Grand Rapids, Michigan: Wm. B. Eerdmans Publishing Company, 1955), 237.

[7] St. Gregory Nazianzen, "Oration VIII: Funeral Oration on His Sister Gorgonia," in *Nicene and Post-Nicene Fathers*, Second Series, Vol. 7., eds. Philip Schaff and Henry Wace (Grand Rapids, Michigan: Wm. B. Eerdmans Publishing Company, 1955), 244.

[8] St. Augustine, *Confessions*, trans. Henry Chadwick (Oxford: Oxford University Press, 2008), 171-172.

[9] St. Augustine, *Confessions*, 172.

[10] Venerable Bede, *The Life and Miracles of St. Cuthbert, Bishop of Lindesfarne*, in *Internet Medieval Sourcebook* (New York: Fordham University, 1999), IV.

[11] St. Teresa of Ávila, *The Life of Teresa of Jesus: The Autobiography of Teresa of Ávila*, trans. E. Allison Peers (New York: Penguin Random House, 1991), 88.

[12] Scott L. Smith, Jr., *Near-Death Experiences* (Nashua, New Hampshire: Sophia Press, 2025), Kindle, 62-63.

[13] Evelyn Elsaesser, *Spontaneous Contacts with the Deceased: A Large-Scale International Survey Reveals the Circumstances, Lived Experience and Beneficial Impact of After-Death Communications* (ADCs) (New York: Iff Books, 2023), Kindle, 22, 36, 82.

[14] Elsaesser.

[15] Bill and Judy Guggenheim, *Hello from Heaven* (New York: Bantam Books, 1997), 171-173.

[16] St. Augustine, *The City of God, Books I-VII*, trans. Gerald G. Walsh and Demetrius B. Zema (Washington, DC: Catholic University of America Press, 2008), 438.

[17] 16 St. Augustine, *City of God*, 450.

[18] Sr. Benedicta Ward, *Miracles and the Medieval Mind: Theory, Record and Event, 1000–1215* (London: Scholar Press, 1982), 321.

[19] Evelyn Underhill, *Mysticism: A Study in the Nature and Development of Spiritual Consciousness* (Mineola, NY: Dover Publications, 2002), 252.

[20] St. Bonaventure, *The Life of St. Francis* (London: The International Society of Franciscan Studies, 1915), 188.

[21] *The Little Flowers of St. Francis*, trans. Roger Hudleston (Whitefish, Wyoming: Literary Licensing, LLC, 2013), 141.

[22] Pope Francis, *Evangelii Gaudium* [Apostolic Exhortation on the Proclamation of the Gospel in Today's World], 265, vatican.va/evangelii-gaudium/en/files/ assets/basic-html/page3.html.

[23] Nancy Evans Bush and Bruce Greyson, "Distressing Near-Death Experiences: The Basics," *Missouri Medicine* 111, no. 6 (2014): 486-491, https://pmc.ncbi.nlm.nih.gov/articles/PMC6173534/.

[24] Venerable Bede, *The Ecclesiastical History of the English Nation*, trans. John Stevens (London: J. M. Dent, 1910), 241-242.

[25] Howard Storm, *My Descent into Death: A Second Chance at Life* (Albuquerque, New Mexico: Harmony, 2005), Kindle, 8.

[26] Storm, 20.

[27] Kevin Williams, "Why Near-Death Experiences Are Not Hallucinations," September 21, 2019, https://near-death.com/why-ndes-are-not-hallucinations/.

[28] Jeffrey Long and Paul Perry, *Evidence of the Afterlife: The Science of Near-Death Experiences* (San Francisco: HarperOne, 2011).

[29] George W. Cornell, "Spiritual Experiences Defy Scientific Beliefs," *Daily News Los Angeles*, January 10, 1987.

[30] "Near-death Experiences Linked to REM Sleep Intrusion on Wakefulness," *Sleep Review*, July 3, 2019, https://sleepreviewmag.com/sleep-health/sleep-whole-body/brain/near-death-experiences-rem-sleep-intrusion/.

[31] Samuel H. Dresner, *Zaddik* (New York: Schocken, 1960), 125.

[32] Robert Lee Hotz, "Religion," *Los Angeles Times*, November 8, 1997.

[33] Walter Brueggemann, *The Prophetic Imagination*, (Minneapolis: Fortress Press, 1978), 79.

[34] Karl Barth, *Church Dogmatics, Vol. IV, The Doctrine of Reconciliation*, Part 3.2, §73, trans. G. W. Bromiley, eds. G. W. Bromiley and T. F. Torrance (New York: T&T Clark International, 1961), 916.

About the Authors

Deacon Eddie Ensley

Deacon Robert Herrman

Eddie Ensley and **Robert Herrmann** are permanent deacons in the Diocese of Savannah. They served on the clergy staff at St. Anne Catholic Church in Columbus, Georgia, and are both Knights of Columbus members of Bishop Gross 1019. Together, they operate Deacons in Ministry, through which they have preached to more than 370,000 people in 350 locations since 2001. Ensley is a licensed clinical pastoral counselor with a master's degree in pastoral studies and a doctorate in clinical pastoral counseling. He serves on the United States Conference of Catholic Bishop committee for healing and understanding of Native Americans. Hermann is certified in parish ministry and is an expert in spiritual journaling and teaching contemplative prayer.

The Word Among Us publishes a monthly devotional magazine, books, Bible studies, and pamphlets that help Catholics grow in their faith.

To learn more about who we are and what we publish, visit www.wau.org. There you will find a variety of Catholic resources that will help you grow in your faith.

Your review makes a difference! If you enjoyed this book, please consider sharing your review on Amazon using the QR code below.

Embrace His Word
Listen to God . . .

www.wau.org

www.ingramcontent.com/pod-product-compliance
Lightning Source LLC
Chambersburg PA
CBHW070116080526
44586CB00013B/1307